Investment Arbitration's Tightrope

Investment Arbitration's Tightrope

Ethics, Power and Responsibility

Paolo Vargiu

ANTHEM PRESS

Anthem Press
An imprint of Wimbledon Publishing Company
www.anthempress.com

This edition first published in UK and USA 2025
by ANTHEM PRESS
75–76 Blackfriars Road, London SE1 8HA, UK
or PO Box 9779, London SW19 7ZG, UK
and
244 Madison Ave #116, New York, NY 10016, USA

British Library Cataloguing-in-Publication Data
A catalogue record for this book is available from the British Library.

Library of Congress Cataloging-in-Publication Data: 2025930166
A catalog record for this book has been requested.

ISBN-13: 978-1-83999-356-5 (Hbk)
ISBN-10: 1-83999-356-1 (Hbk)

Cover Credit: Javardh/Upsplash

This title is also available as an e-book.

CONTENTS

ACKNOWLEDGEMENTS

This monograph stands as the endpoint (or at least a resting place) of a journey both protracted and intermittently discordant. There were times when I doubted it would ever emerge into the world, weighed down as it is by a subject, such as investment arbitration, currently caught in the crosscurrents of scrutiny and revision. Not that I seriously believe the system of investment arbitration will undergo anything resembling substantive reform; systems of such ilk rarely do. Yet, somehow, I completed my task. As is customary – in fact, practically obligatory in our circles – the acknowledgements page brims with names, a ritual that is as much a professional necessity as a gesture of gratitude. In this case, however, the thanks are genuine, as many individuals and institutions contributed in ways I am truly beholden to, despite the inevitable sense that such debts are, by their nature, only ever incompletely repaid.

Foremost among my debts of gratitude are those owed to my colleagues at Leicester Law School, whose blend of encouragement, perceptiveness and camaraderie has lent both substance and structure to my research. Of particular note are the contributions of Tony Cole, Katja Ziegler, Pascale Lorber, Eugenia Caracciolo Di Torella, Adam Cygan, Pablo Cortes, Peter Cumper and Stephen Riley, whose guidance – dispensed with an admirable mix of tact and forthrightness – proved indispensable. It is not too much to say that their interventions spared this work from certain missteps that might otherwise have gone unchecked.

Particular thanks are due to my friends and colleagues within the IEL Collective, whose expertise and generosity have been instrumental in shaping this work, although they might be surprised to learn how often their offhand remarks were taken as definitive wisdom. I am especially indebted to Celine Tan, Anil Yilmaz Vastardis, Annamaria La Chimia, Daria Davitti, Mavluda Sattorova, Jean Ho, Serena Natile, David Schneiderman and Tara Van Ho, whose mentorship and scholarship have been a constant source of inspiration, as well as a gentle reminder that even the most brilliant ideas benefit from a dash of pragmatism (and occasionally a second draft).

A number of other colleagues, whether they realised it at the time or not, have been indispensable in ensuring that this book reached its conclusion. I would like to thank Martins Paparinskis, Vincenzo Pacillo, Tarcisio Gazzini, Stelios Andreadakis, Francesco Seatzu, Albert Sanchez-Graells, Meagan Wong, Giulia Ciliberto and Daniele Amoroso. Their contributions ranged from timely advice to what I can only describe as unwitting acts of support, though I suspect some may now wish they had claimed royalties instead.

On a personal note, I must thank my family for their unwavering support and remarkable patience throughout the many twists and turns of this demanding project. Their belief in me, sometimes more robust than my own, has been a constant source of strength and, at crucial moments, the gentle prod needed to keep going, even when I might have preferred to abandon my notes in favour of more sociable pursuits. A particularly heartfelt thank you must go to my wife, Arianna, whose patience, insight and unfailing good humour have been the quiet foundation upon which this work was built. Her capacity to endure the peculiar rhythms of my academic obsession – with its late nights and occasional bouts of unwarranted self-importance – deserves far more recognition than a mere acknowledgement here. It is no exaggeration to say that, without her steady presence and sharp perspective, both this book and my very life would be considerably poorer.

Leicester, 30 June 2024

The job of judges is to apply the law,
not to indulge their personal preferences.

Tom Bingham

Rigore è quando arbitro fischia.

Vujadin Boškov

Chapter 1

INTRODUCTION

The role of investment arbitrators has been the subject of close and intense scrutiny in recent years.[1] The purposes of such scrutiny were not necessarily theoretical or academic: the sudden and dramatic surge in interest of investment arbitration was in fact part of the more general backlash against

---

[1] See among others Puig and Strezhnev, 'Testing Cognitive Bias: Experimental Approaches and Investment Arbitration', 85–99; Lie, 'The Influence of Law Firms in Investment Arbitration', 100–132; Giorgetti, 'Arbitrator Challenges in International Investment Tribunals', 133–158; Kapeliuk, 'Dissents in Investment Arbitration: On Collegiality and Individualism', 159–168; Fabri and Stoppioni, *International Investment Law – An Analysis of the Major Decisions* parts I and II; Grant and Kieff, 'Appointing Arbitrators: Tenure, Public Confidence, and a Middle Road for ISDS Reform', 171–239; Vargiu, 'Stakeholders of Investment Arbitration: establishing a dialogue among arbitrators, states, investors, academics and other actors in international investment law', 5–25; Lorfing and Nanteuil, 'Projet de code de conduite pour les arbitres dans les différends relatifs aux investissements internationaux – version deux', 581–585; Potestà, 'Appointment of Arbitrators in the Changing ISDS Landscape', 231–239; Simões, 'Investment Arbitration and the Chimera of an Ideal Adjudicative Community', 687–704; Díaz, *El árbitro en el sistema CIADI: estudio acerca de la independencia, imparcialidad, deberes, derechos y responsabilidad de los árbitros CIADI*; Stefano, 'From arbitrators to judges? reflections on the reform of investor-State dispute settlement', 137–161; Cowe, '"It's not me, it's you': Arbitrator's Conduct and the Public's Opinion of ISDS', 251–262; Gómez, *Key Duties of International Investment Arbitrators: a Transnational Study of Legal and Ethical Dilemmas*; Zárate, 'Nineteenth Century Arbitrators' Powers – Has There Been Any Progress to Date?', 217–235; Bjorklund, 'Are Arbitrators (Judicial) Activists?', 49–60; Harten, 'Leaders in the Expansive and Restrictive Interpretation of Investment Treaties: A Descriptive Study of ISDS Awards to 2010', 507–549; Bentolila, *Arbitrators as Lawmakers*; Cotula and Perrone, 'Seeing Santurbán through ISDS: A sociolegal case study of Eco Oro v. Colombia', 440–461; Faccio, 'Investment Contracts and the Reform of Investment Arbitration: Towards Sustainability', 625–643; Heath, 'Investment Arbitration and State-Driven Reform: New Treaties, Old Outcomes', 717–721; Alschner, *Investment Arbitration and State-Driven Reform: New Treaties, Old Outcomes.*

investment arbitration that emerged – perhaps rightfully – in the last decade.[2] Questions about the legitimacy of investment arbitration,[3] the foundations of the process,[4] the appropriateness of the applicable law in a world that is radically different from the one in which the earliest bilateral investment treaties (BITs) were drafted and signed,[5] have sparked a vivid (although mostly academic, until the establishment of the Working Group III by UNCITRAL)[6] discussion on whether investment arbitration is still a mechanism fit to settle disputes between foreign investors and host states. Indeed, the first of the contemporary BITs had been signed in a world where geographic distances often marked the breadth of the cultural distances between the signatory states; it was a world in which investing abroad carried significant risks for a company, beyond that of seeing their assets nationalised or the common business risks associated with any economic enterprise.[7] In such a world, BITs offered a layer of protection for businesses abroad that general international law was not considered capable to provide.

---

2 The topic is addressed in greater detail in Chapter 4.1. See also Lindseth, 'Theorizing Backlash: Supranational Governance and International Investment Law and Arbitration in Comparative Perspective', 34–70; Langford and Behn, 'Managing Backlash: The Evolving Investment Treaty Arbitrator?', 551–580; Waibel, Kaushal, Chung, and Balchin, *The Backlash against Investment Arbitration: Perceptions and Reality*.

3 A rather comprehensive overview of these concerns is provided in Behn, Fauchald, and Langford (eds.), *The Legitimacy of Investment Arbitration: Empirical Perspectives*, *supra* note 1; Butler, 'Human Rights in International Commercial and Investment Arbitration', 139–185; Bungenberg, 'Democracy and International Investment Law', 186–210; Reinisch, 'Investment Arbitration and the Rule of Law', 211–243; Bjorklund, 'The Legitimacy of the International Centre for Settlement of Investment Disputes', 234–283; Sweet and Grisel, *The Evolution of International Arbitration: Judicialization, Governance, Legitimacy*.

4 See *ex multis* Delimatsis, Dimitropoulos, and Gourgourinis, *State Capitalism and International Investment Law*; Salacuse, *The Three Laws of International Investment: National, Contractual, and International Frameworks for Foreign Capital*.

5 See in particular Kjos, *Applicable Law in Investor-State Arbitration: The Interplay between National and International Law*; Dumberry, *A Guide to General Principles of Law in International Investment Arbitration*; Zarra, 'Applicable Law in Investment Arbitration: the 2021 Practice', 391–420; Giardina, 'International Investment Arbitration: Recent Developments as to the Applicable Law and Unilateral Recourse', 29–39; and for an interesting take on an often overlooked issue in the applicable law to investment dispute Sipiorski, *Good Faith in International Investment Arbitration*.

6 All the documents on the works of the UNCITRAL Working Group III (Investor-State Dispute Settlement Reform) are available at https://uncitral.un.org/en/working_groups/3/investor-state.

7 I would like to refer the readership to the seminal Vandevelde, *The First Bilateral Investment Treaties: U.S. Postwar Friendship, Commerce, and Navigation Treaties*.

The globalised society we currently live in, however, is radically different from the fragmented and still partly colonial world that led to the first BITs. Geographical distances are now far easier to cover; cultural distances are still present, but the Internet, the relative easiness of travelling, the presence of foreign students in most universities, and other similar factors have made it 'normal' for most companies to plan for expansions and development abroad.[8] There is, however, one thing that has not changed since states started to regulate the relationship between their national investors and their governments via bilateral treaties: natural resources remain scarce, and they are still mostly located in developing countries.[9] Moreover, developing countries are now seen not only as places to conduct physical investment – as in mining or building roads or rails, for instance – but also as markets like any other.[10] A market is an opportunity for expansion and growth: this is the reason why even companies in the tertiary sector have begun investing abroad, and attempted (often successfully) to enjoy the protection offered by BITs. The world might be globalised, but investment law has not really reacted to these changes. Granted, the most recent BITs are rather sophisticated instruments, unlike the very basic treaties that for decades have characterised the regulation of foreign investment;[11] moreover, BITs are no longer signed between a developed and

8 The literature on the emergence and increased importance of multinational corporation in global business is rather extensive, encompassing a wide range of studies and different perspectives. Due to the sheer volume of work in this field, only a few key contributions can be highlighted to illustrate the primary advancements and foundational theories; in particular I would like to refer to Brennan, *Enacting Globalization: Multidisciplinary Perspectives on International Integration*; Ferreira, 'Intertwined paths of globalization and international investment law', 85–99; Byrnes, Hayashi, and Michaelsen, *International Law in the New Age of Globalization*.

9 Bastos, 'A Southern African Approach to the Permanent Sovereignty over Natural Resources and Common Resource Management Systems', 61–78; Bruch, Muffett and Nichols, *Governance, Natural Resources and Post-conflict Peacebuilding*; Jacur, Bonfanti, and Seatzu, *Natural Resources Grabbing: An International Law Perspective*.

10 See e.g. Jamali and Karam, 'Corporate social responsibility in developing countries as an emerging field of study', 32–61; Naudé, 'Entrepreneurship, developing countries, and development economics: new approaches and insights', 1–12.

11 A few recent examples are the 2023 Bulgaria Model BIT, available at https://investmentpolicy.unctad.org/international-investment-agreements/treaty-files/8421/download; the 2022 Italy Model BIT, at https://investmentpolicy.unctad.org/international-investment-agreements/treaty-files/6438/download; the 2019 Morocco Model BIT, at https://investmentpolicy.unctad.org/international-investment-agreements/treaty-files/5895/download; and the whole tradition of BITs commenced with the 2004 US Model BIT, available at https://investmentpolicy.unctad.org/international-investment-agreements/treaty-files/2872/download. See also Salacuse, *The Law of Investment Treaties*.

a developing country, as the number of so-called 'South–South' BITs has increased exponentially since the beginning of the century.[12] However, in spite of such sophistication and the increase of investment relationships between developing countries, the main features of BITs remain largely the same as ever: the main standards of protection continue to be the Fair and Equitable Treatment, the National Treatment, the Most Favoured Nation treatment and the obligation to provide full protection and security to aliens abroad.[13] Expropriation also remains regulated by general international law, and attempts to modify such a regime – perhaps removing the requirement that nationalisation not be arbitrary – have been less than successful.[14] And, last but certainly not least, investment arbitration maintains its status as the chief instrument for the settlement of disputes between investors and host states.[15]

It is interesting to note, in this regard, that, unlike BITs, investment arbitration has not really changed much since the first case was brought before a tribunal constituted under the aegis of the International Centre for the Settlement of

12 The development of South–South Bilateral Investment Treaties (BITs) has been a significant trend in international economic relations, reflecting the growing economic interdependence among developing countries. These treaties aim to promote and protect investments between countries of the Global South, facilitating mutual economic growth and development. Over the years, South–South BITs have evolved to address specific needs and concerns of developing economies, such as fair treatment of investors, dispute resolution mechanisms and sustainable development goals. See in particular Poulsen, The Significance of South-South BITs for the International Investment Regime: A Quantitative Analysis, 101–130; Sornarajah, *The International Law on Foreign Investment*, 291–339; Mota, *Foreign Investment and Investment Arbitration in Asia.*

13 See generally Newcombe and Paradell, *Law and Practice of Investment Treaties: Standards of Treatment*; Reinisch, *Standards of Investment Protection*; Reinisch and Schreuer, *International Protection of Investments: The Substantive Standards*; Reinisch and Schill, *Investment Protection Standards and the Rule of Law.*

14 The Southern African Development Community (SADC) Model Bilateral Investment Treaty (BIT), available at https://www.iisd.org/itn/wp-content/uploads/2012/10/sadc-model-bit-template-final.pdf, was developed to provide a comprehensive framework for investment protection and promotion among its member states. Despite its detailed provisions aimed at balancing investor rights and state regulatory autonomy, however, the SADC Model BIT has yet to be used in practice. See Vargiu and Seatzu, 'Africanizing Bilateral Investment Treaties ('BITs'): Some Case Studies and Future Prospects of a Pro-Active African Approach to International Investment', 143–168; Vargiu and Seatzu, 'Bilateralism, Multilateralism and the Quest for a Multilateral Investment Agreement for Sub-Saharan African Countries', 315–340.

15 See generally Schill and Vidigal, 'Designing investment dispute settlement à la carte: insights from comparative institutional design analysis', 314–344.

Investment Disputes (hereinafter referred to as 'ICSID').[16] From a procedural perspective, investment arbitration is still subject to the same rules – slightly amended over the years – and especially to the principles laid down in articles 36 to 55 of the ICSID Convention.[17] Substantively, however, it may be said that the role of the arbitrators has expanded over the years. While Section 3 of the Convention grants extensive powers to arbitrators from the perspective of the procedures to be followed, both the Convention and the Arbitration Rules are silent as to the extent to which arbitrators can interpret the applicable law.[18] On one hand, such silence and the *quasi*-judicial nature of their role should call for caution in their interpretive efforts, precluding operations that result in law-making rather than interpretation; on the other hand, the vagueness of the provisions of many BITs, and the necessity of interpretation, have led to an increase in significance of the role of investment arbitrators. The need for interpretation in particular, whether consistent or not, has progressively led to the establishment of a *de facto* system of precedent in investment arbitration.[19] Not only it is now customary to find copious and detailed references to previous cases in any ICSID award, but it is also becoming progressively rarer to find divergent interpretations of the main principles governing the international law on foreign investment. One might not need to think farther than the

16 Convention on the Settlement of Investment Disputes between States and Nationals of Other States (ICSID Convention), 18 March 1965, 575 U.N.T.S. 159. See generally Parra, *The History of ICSID*.

17 Specifically, the Articles on the Request for Arbitration (36), the Constitution of the Tribunal (37–40), the Powers and Functions of the Tribunal (41–47), the Award (48–49), the Interpretation, Revision and Annulment of the Award (50–52) and the Recognition and Enforcement of the Award (53–55).

18 Article 42 of the ICSID Convention merely states that the Tribunal will resolve a dispute based on the legal rules agreed upon by the parties involved; if no such agreement exists, the Tribunal will apply the law of the Contracting State that is a party to the dispute, including its conflict of law rules, along with any relevant international law. The Tribunal is not permitted to refrain from making a decision due to ambiguities or gaps in the law; however, if the parties consent, the Tribunal retains the authority to resolve the dispute based on principles of equity and fairness (*ex aequo et bono*).

19 *Infra*, 3.2. In investment arbitration, a de facto system of precedent has emerged, where arbitral tribunals often refer to and rely on previous decisions to ensure consistency and predictability in their rulings. Although not formally binding, these precedents influence the development of investment law by guiding tribunals in interpreting similar legal issues and principles across different cases. See in particular Reed, 'The "De Facto" Precedent Regime in Investment Arbitration: a Case for Proactive Case Management', 95–103; Chen, 'Precedent and dialogue in investment treaty arbitration', 47–94; Vargiu, '*Langue* and *Parole* of Investment Law', 293–312.

Salini criteria: developed to provide a modicum of guidance to arbitral tribunals vested with the question of whether an economic activity was to be considered an investment under international law, the *Salini* criteria have quickly become a factually mandatory standard, to the point that even tribunals outside of the ICSID system have considered themselves under the obligation of applying the criteria to the enquiry on whether or not the dispute before them was based on an investment.[20] The *Salini* criteria might be the most striking example of how the activism of arbitrators has, in practice, created new law, even in contradiction with what the *travaux preparatoires* show in terms of the intention of the drafters that regard to the definition of investment.[21] However, similar considerations may be made with regard to most of the standards and rules commonly applied in investment arbitration.[22] As previously mentioned, the

---

20 Salini Costruttori S.p.A. and Italstrade S.p.A. v. Kingdom of Morocco [I], ICSID Case No. ARB/00/4, Decision on Jurisdiction, 31 July 2001. Among the many scholarly contributions on the *Salini* criteria see in particular Vargiu, 'Beyond Hallmarks and Formal Requirements: a "Jurisprudence Constante" on the Notion of Investment in the ICSID Convention', 753–768; Chan and Lai, 'Two decades after Salini v Morocco: the case for retaining the Salini test with modifications', 63–84; Martin, 'Definition of "Investment": Could a Persistent Objector to the Salini Tests be Found in ICSID Arbitral Practice?'; Petsche, 'The Application of the Salini Test Beyond Article 25 of the ICSID Convention: Analysis of Recent Trends in Treaty and Arbitral Practice', 879–906; Petsche, *The Concept of Investment in ICSID Arbitration*; Fellenbaum, 'Putting the Needle to the Salini Bubble?', 103–151; Grabowski, 'The Definition of Investment under the ICSID Convention: A Defense of Salini', 287–309; Banifatemi and Gaillard, 'The Long March towards a Jurisprudence Constante on the Notion of Investment, Salini v. Morocco, ICSID Case No ARB/00/4', 97–125; Burger, 'The Trouble with Salini (Criticism of and Alternatives to the Famous Test)', 521–536; Yala, 'The Notion of "Investment" in ICSID Case Law: a Drifting Jurisdictional Requirement? Some "Un-Conventional" Thoughts on Salini, SGS and Mihaly', 105–126; Wali, 'A Contemporary Evaluation of Decisions and Approaches Shaping the Conceptualization of an "ICSID Investment" ', 224–257.

21 In the preliminary discussions on the ICSID Convention, a definition of investment was initially proposed. Article 30 of the first draft defined 'investment' as 'any contribution of money or other assets of economic value for an indefinite period or, if the period is defined, for not less than five years.' However, this definition was deemed too broad by some delegates and criticized for arbitrarily excluding economic operations lasting less than five years. Others supported including specific categories of investment in the Convention, allowing states to define the term through bilateral or multilateral agreements. Ultimately, these proposals were also rejected. See Schreuer, Malintoppi, Reinisch, and Sinclair, *The ICSID Convention: A Commentary* 82–85.

22 See IBRD, The Convention on the Settlement of Investment Disputes, Documents Concerning the Origin and the Formulation of the Convention (ICSID History), Vols. i and ii in particular.

activism of arbitrators has not been a self-developed approach, but it has rather been made necessary by the paucity of definitions and explanations in the BITs of the first generation.[23] One might argue that the more recent BITs are much more detailed and precise in certain definitions; this, paired with the content of various rules and principles developed over the years in the case-law, would entail the progressive reduction of the role of arbitrators: indeed, if BITs are now more precise, and there is a robust body of case-law to assist them, arbitrators would not need to be as active in interpreting the applicable law as they used to. However, as it will be explained in the remainder of this book, such 'arbitral activism' that has become a sort of custom in investment arbitration; and the dramatic increase, in the ranks of investment arbitrators, of practitioners with very solid experience in commercial arbitration but little familiarity with public international law, has led to further activism, rather creative interpretations of treaties, and maintaining the prominence of arbitrators in the process.

Such prominence, however, cannot but come with certain responsibilities. Investment arbitration, as it is now well known, was aptly defined as 'mixed' international arbitration.[24] Indeed, even though investment arbitration replicates many of the features of commercial arbitration, the presence of a state – thus a public law entity – makes it necessary to adapt the procedure to the fact that one of the parties to the dispute is a sovereign body. Arbitrators, too, must adapt their behaviour to the requirements of what is, in essence, a public law process – notwithstanding its undeniable similarities with a private system of administration of justice like commercial arbitration. Some of such

---

23 Arbitral activism in investment arbitration refers to the phenomenon where arbitrators take a proactive role in interpreting and applying the law, often extending beyond a narrow interpretation of the treaty provisions and the parties' intentions. This approach can lead to the creation of new legal principles or the broadening of existing ones, significantly influencing the development of international investment law. While arbitral activism can enhance the dynamism and adaptability of the arbitration process, it also raises concerns regarding the legitimacy and predictability of arbitral decisions, as it may be perceived as undermining state sovereignty and the stability of the legal framework governing international investments. Alcolea, 'Arbitral Activism and Choice of Law under the ICSID Convention', 499–546.

24 This term comes from the historically seminal book by Toope, *Mixed International Arbitration: Studies in Arbitration between States and Private Persons.* The definition in question underscores the fact that investment arbitration involves parties from different legal and national backgrounds, typically a private investor and a sovereign state, and its hybrid nature combines elements of public international law, which governs the state's conduct, with private international law, which pertains to the investor's rights and obligations.

adaptations are expressly required by specific rules and principles in the ICSID Convention;[25] others are contingent on the sovereign nature of states, who do not lose such sovereignty even when the subject themselves to a process, such as that of arbitration, that has many similarities, as stated beforehand, with a private dispute settlement mechanism.[26] Other adaptations, however, might be necessary not only because of the public law nature of one of the parties to the dispute but also to temperate somehow the inherent inequalities of investment arbitration.[27]

As it has been briefly mentioned, investment arbitration is a by-product of a legal imagination that dates back to the 1950s and 1960s, pioneering years in which the undeniable differences in economic power between developed and developing countries (or, more correctly, between Western capital exporting states and newly independent postcolonial states) justified to a certain extent the establishment of a dispute settlement mechanism specifically designed to protect the interests of one party only.[28] Indeed, an investment arbitration can

---

25 See the afore-mentioned Article 42(1) of the ICSID Convention ('The Tribunal shall decide a dispute in accordance with such rules of law as may be agreed by the parties. In the absence of such agreement, the Tribunal shall apply the law of the Contracting State party to the dispute (including its rules on the conflict of laws) and such rules of international law as may be applicable.'

26 May I refer the reader to the rather interesting insights gathered in Huerta-Goldman, Romanetti, and Stirnimann, *WTO Litigation, Investment Arbitration, and Commercial Arbitration.*

27 See among others Maria Laura Marceddu, Pietro Ortolani, 'What is wrong with investment arbitration? Evidence from a set of behavioural experiments', 31(2) *European Journal of International Law* 405–428 (2020); Daniel Behn, Malcolm Langford, Laura Létourneau-Tremblay, 'Empirical perspectives on investment arbitration: what do we know? Does it matter?', 21(2) *The Journal of World Investment and Trade* 188–250 (2020); Anil Yilmaz Vastardis, Gus Van Harten, 'Critiques of Investment Arbitration Reform: An Introduction', 24(3) *The Journal of World Investment and Trade* 363–371 (2023); Nitish Monebhurrun, Carolina Olarte-Bácares, Marco A. Velásquez-Ruiz, *International Investment Law and Arbitration from a Latin American Perspective*, Springer, 2024; Mavluda Sattorova, 'Return to the Local Remedies Rule in European BITs? Power (Inequalities), Dispute Settlement, and Change in Investment Treaty Law', 39(2) *Legal Issues of Economic Integration* 223–247 (2012).

28 Perrone, *Investment Treaties and the Legal Imagination: How Foreign Investors Play by their Own Rules.* The title of Perrone's book reminds to James Boyd White's concept of *The Legal Imagination* (University of Chicago Press, 1973), which refers to the capacity of lawyers and legal thinkers to creatively and interpretively engage with legal texts, principles, and practices. White in particular underscored the role of narrative, rhetoric, and interpretation in the law, suggesting that practitioners and adjudicators do not merely apply rules mechanically, but actively shape and reshape the law through their imaginative engagement.

only nominally be won by the respondent state. Even though the recognition of the correctness of the behaviour of the state under international law, and the subsequent denial of damages claimed by the foreign investor, would certainly be welcomed by any state sitting on the respondent's seat, such an outcome should probably be labelled as 'not losing' rather than winning. States have very little to gain from being involved in an investment arbitral process. Globalisation, the emergence of previously unimaginably large multinational corporations the power of which often trumps that of states (including some developed countries), and the rise of movements that denunciated the fact that investment law (and investment arbitration) might not be the most fitting instrument for poorer countries' economic and development needs, are all factors that contribute to questioning whether investment law, rather than an instrument of justice, could in fact be a tool for the perpetuation of global inequalities. Investment law, however, is to be found as much in treaties as in the outcome of the interpretive efforts of arbitrators; in fact, as mentioned beforehand, some principles are entirely derived from the case-law rather than treaties. One might argue, therefore, that arbitrators cannot simply be identified as administrators of justice. The significance of their interpretive effort is as such as to elevate them to *de facto* lawmakers.[29] If that is the case, though, what are the actual responsibilities, from a practical as well as an ethical perspective, of arbitrators – besides the professional requirements and what is stated in the ICSID Convention – and do they play a role in balancing the powers at play in investment arbitration?

This question is the core of the inquiry carried on in this book. From a technical standpoint, the role of investment arbitrators has been discussed extensively. The most prominent volumes on investment arbitration, however, address the problem from a practitioner-oriented perspective, focusing on the legal requirements to act as arbitrators and how their duties must be carried out with respect to the particular dispute they are appointed to hear.[30]

29 Bentolila, *Arbitrators as Lawmakers*, *supra* note 1; Popova, Seifert, 'Gatekeeping, Lawmaking, and Rulemaking: Lessons from Third-Party Funding in Investment Arbitration', *supra* note 1, 133–155. An interesting and fresh perspective is offered by Zekos, *Judges and Arbitrators as Law Makers. Advanced Artificial Intelligence and Robo-Justice* 53–87.

30 That is the case, for instance, of McLachlan, Shore, and Weiniger, *International Investment Arbitration: Substantive Principles*; or Dahlquist and Hober, *Investment Treaty Arbitration: Problems and Exercises*. Closer to the perspective of this research is Eric De Brabandere's 'Investment treaty arbitration as public international law: procedural aspects and implications', Cambridge University Press, 2016, which underscores the public international law nature of investment arbitration against

This book, instead, represents an attempt to expand such debate onto whether the duties of arbitrators extend beyond their disputes – and, if so, why and how. The inquiry shall start with an overview of the fundamental principles that guide the behaviour and responsibilities of investment arbitrators. Chapter 2 begins by examining the importance of impartiality and independence, highlighting the necessity for arbitrators to remain unbiased and free from any conflict of interest. The discussion then shifts to the applicable law and its application, providing insights into how arbitrators interpret and implement relevant legal frameworks. Further, the chapter addresses the requisite knowledge and expertise, underscoring the need for arbitrators to possess a deep understanding of both legal- and sector-specific matters. Confidentiality is also explored, emphasising the obligation of arbitrators to maintain the privacy of proceedings and sensitive information. Finally, the chapter concludes with an analysis of the powers conferred upon arbitrators by Article 44 of the ICSID Convention, detailing the scope and limitations of their authority in conducting arbitration proceedings.

The following chapter abandons the practice-oriented approach of Chapter 2 to look at the functions actually performed by arbitrators in the global context of investment law, exploring the broader roles and responsibilities of arbitrators outside the immediate context of resolving disputes. Chapter 3 begins with a discussion on interpretation, examining how arbitrators approach the task of interpreting legal texts and treaty provisions. The chapter then addresses the *de facto* doctrine of precedent in international investment law, analysing how past arbitral decisions influence subsequent cases despite the lack of a formal precedent system. Lastly, the chapter questions the importance of stating the reasons upon which an award is based, emphasising the need for transparency and clarity in arbitral decision-making to ensure the legitimacy and acceptability of the awards rendered.

---

the increasing influence of interpretive principles and standards of conduct of commercial arbitration. De Brabandere's book, however, while sharing a similar approach, is focused on the relevant public law issues, such as, amongst others, personal requirements of arbitrators, applicable law, or transparency; it does not address the responsibilities of arbitrators as de facto international lawmakers and the ethical questions related to it. The closest work currently on the market is Katia Fach Gómez, 'Key duties of international investment arbitrators: a transnational study of legal and ethical dilemmas', *supra*, note 1. Fach Gómez's book, however, is a critical investigation, from an ethics perspective, on the duties of arbitrators within the context of the disputes they are hearing.

Chapter 4 is then aimed at bridging the gap between the duties described in Chapter 2 and the responsibilities theorized in Chapter 3. In this perspective, the chapter addresses the evolving responsibilities of arbitrators in the context of investment arbitration and the challenges they face, starting from an examination of the afore-mentioned backlash against investment arbitration, and discussing the criticisms and concerns raised by various stakeholders regarding its fairness and legitimacy. Following this, the chapter presents a defence of investment arbitration, outlining the arguments in support of its continued relevance and effectiveness. The discussion then shifts to the problem with the applicable law, exploring the complexities and issues associated with determining and applying the correct legal framework. To conclude, the chapter considers what could be asked of arbitrators, suggesting ways in which arbitrators can adapt and improve their practices to better meet the demands and expectations of the international investment community. Finally, Chapter 5, besides the customary summary of the findings, provides a few concluding remarks on the analysis carried out in this book.

Chapter 2

PRINCIPLES GOVERNING THE CONDUCT OF INVESTMENT ARBITRATORS

2.1. Preliminary Remarks

To a certain extent, the duties of investment arbitrators do not substantially differ from those of commercial arbitrators. Indeed, the proceedings are remarkably similar, and, as will be seen in this chapter, there is a significant overlap between what is required of commercial arbitrators and what is necessary, in terms of personal and professional qualifications, to sit in an ICSID tribunal or in another arbitral tribunal hearing a dispute between an investor and a host state. Independence, impartiality and respecting the confidentiality of proceedings are all characteristics of any arbitrator, regardless of the nature of the dispute brought before them.[1] While the literature on these aspects (especially impartiality and independence) is sufficiently developed, the personal qualities of investment arbitrators have been seldom discussed in the context of a tribunal; and even though the international commercial arbitral case-law is slightly richer in instances in which the personal characteristics of arbitrators have been addressed, the confidentiality of arbitral awards makes it quite hard to conduct a systematic

1 See comparatively Angoura, *The Impartiality and Independence of Arbitrators in International Commercial Arbitration*; Cleis, *The Independence and Impartiality of ICSID Arbitrators: Current Case Law, Alternative Approaches, and Improvement Suggestions*; Bělohlávek, Rozehnalová, and Černý, *Independence and Impartiality of Arbitrators*; Haersolte-van Hof, 'Impartiality and independence: fundamental and fluid', 599–611; Rubins, Lauterburg, 'Independence, Impartiality and Duty of Disclosure in Investment Arbitration', 153–180.

study of what are all the principles applicable to the conduct of an arbitrator.[2] There is, moreover, no explicit provision in the ICSID Convention – or, in fact, in other international law instruments – analytically addressing the principles governing the conduct of investment arbitrators. The International Centre for the Settlement of Investment Disputes (ICSID) and the United Nations Commission on International Trade Law (UNCITRAL) have jointly developed a Code of Conduct for Arbitrators in International Investment Disputes, which establishes principles and guidelines to ensure arbitrators' independence and impartiality, as well as their obligation to conduct proceedings with integrity, fairness, efficiency and respect. The Code is derived from a comparative analysis of standards set forth in existing codes of conduct in investment treaties, arbitration rules for investment disputes and practices of international courts.[3] The Code of Conduct, however, is still quite recent, and remains an instrument of soft law[4]; the principles governing the conduct of investment arbitrators are thus still to be identified from a plurality of sources. With regard to the ICSID context, one might not look further than the Convention, the Arbitration rules and the cases in which arbitrators have been challenged by one of the parties. For what concerns *ad hoc* tribunals, a

---

2 On the confidentiality of international commercial arbitration may I refer the reader to Reymond-Eniaeva, *Towards a Uniform Approach to Confidentiality of International Commercial Arbitration* Smeureanu, *Confidentiality in International Commercial Arbitration*; Foden and Repousis, 'Giving away home field advantage: the misguided attack on confidentiality in international commercial arbitration', 401–418; Trakman, 'Confidentiality in international commercial arbitration', 1–18; Blavi, 'A Case in Favour of Publicity Available Awards in International Commercial Arbitration: Transparency v. Confidentiality', 83–92; Malatesta, 'Confidentiality in International Commercial Arbitration', 39–51; Pislevik, 'Precedent and development of law: Is it time for greater transparency in International Commercial Arbitration?', 241–260.

3 UNCITRAL Code of Conduct for Arbitrators in International Investment Dispute Resolution, available at https://uncitral.un.org/sites/uncitral.un.org/files/media-documents/uncitral/en/2318944_coc_arbitrators_e-book_eng.pdf. Further documents on the Code of Conduct can be found on the ICSID website at https://icsid.worldbank.org/resources/code-of-conduct.

4 On the significance of soft law in arbitration see Dasser, '*Soft law' in International Commercial Arbitration*; Newman and Radine, *Soft Law in International Arbitration*; Mourre, 'Soft law as a condition for the development of trust in international arbitration', 82–98; Marisi, 'Independence and Impartiality: the Role of Soft Law in International Arbitration', 326–345; Korzum, 'Enforcing soft law in international investment arbitration', 1–65; Rosenfeld, 'The Hardening of Soft Law in International Arbitration', 19–36; Álvarez, 'Reviewing the Use of "Soft Law" in Investment Arbitration', 149–200; Schill, 'Sources of international investment law: multilateralization, arbitral precedent, comparativism, soft law', 1095–1115.

similar operation can be made upon the arbitration rules chosen by parties to regulate the proceedings. Moreover, it is to be pointed out that, even prior to the UNCITRAL Code of Conduct, the European Union had expressed a clear position on the necessary ethical and professional requirements of investment arbitrators.[5] Without extending this research to the professional and ethical requirements that one must satisfy in order to practice law in their own country, it is, however, appropriate to look at what the International Bar Association (IBA) guidelines provide in terms of the personal qualities of an arbitrator. Indeed, while not formally binding, the IBA guidelines have long represented the standard to which lawyers at the international level must adhere to; and, in spite of their lack of binding force, they are extremely helpful to shed light on what sorts of qualities an individual must possess in order to serve as an investment arbitrator.[6]

Notwithstanding these developments, however, the way the duties of investment arbitrators are codified – be it in treaties or more or less formal codes of conduct – is hardly systemic. Duties (and often powers) are expressed quite vaguely and at times ambiguously, as will be seen in the remainder of this chapter. On one hand, this is an issue that has traditionally affected a number of investment agreements and has in fact been one of the core

5 The European Commission issued in October 2023 a 'Non-Paper' containing Model Clauses with Annotations to guide EU Member States in negotiating BITs with non-EU countries, available at https://bit.ly/4bVx3Oh. While 'non-papers' do not reflect an official stance of the Commission, the Model Clauses serve as recommendations for Member States' BITs. The Model Clause on the conduct of arbitrators is composed of three paragraphs. Paragraph 1 establishes the principle of arbitrators' independence, detailing behaviours they should avoid and referencing the Code of Conduct, which specifies these behaviours more thoroughly. Paragraph 2 outlines the procedure for challenging an arbitrator who a disputing party believes does not meet the independence requirements specified in Paragraph 1 or the Code of Conduct. The parties involved must agree on an external authority to make a final decision on the challenge, typically a respected and impartial figure such as the President of the International Court of Justice. Paragraph 3 describes the procedure and timelines for issuing a decision on the challenge, unless the arbitrator in question chooses to resign from the tribunal, in which case no decision is needed.

6 Reference is made to the IBA Guidelines on Conflicts of Interest in International Arbitration, available at https://www.ibanet.org/document?id=Guidelines-on-Conflicts-of-Interest-in-International-Arbitration-2024; the IBA Rules on the Taking of Evidence in International Arbitration, available at https://www.ibanet.org/MediaHandler?id=def0807b-9fec-43ef-b624-f2cb2af7cf7b; and the old IBA Rules of Ethics for International Arbitrators, available at https://www.ibanet.org/document?id=Rules-of-ethics-for-international-arbitrators. See *infra*, Chapter 2.1.

factors that led to the activism of arbitrators in their interpretive efforts.[7] As such vagueness extends – at least to a certain degree – to the provisions on the duties of arbitrators, it can be affirmed that there is little clarity, besides the obvious requirements of impartiality, independence and confidentiality, as to the extent of such duties. On the other hand, public international law is characterised by a number of tribunals, from the International Court of Justice (ICJ) to the smaller, treaty-specific tribunals, the judges of which are subject to personal and professional requirements as well as rather specific duties.[8] One might argue that the similar roles played by international arbitrators and adjudicators might allow for analogies in the identification and descriptions of the former's duties on the basis of the latter's. As long as one considers the risks inherent in such an operation, the said analogies might nonetheless help define the duties of arbitrators. This is for what concerns the public international law aspects of international investment disputes; as to the procedural duties of arbitrators, as mentioned beforehand, there is a plurality of sources at play that make the definition of arbitrators' duties quite a challenging task. It has been argued that the UNCITRAL might be the most suitable for room for an organic systematization of arbitrators' duties.[9] In principle, this is certainly agreeable: the UNCITRAL has already introduced paramount instruments that have affected for better investment arbitration (for example, the recent Rules on Transparency in Treaty-based Investor-State Arbitration).[10] However, it seems as though the UNCITRAL prefers to tackle each issue separately, coming up with topic-specific instruments that do little in terms of organising, codifying and

7 See *supra*, Chapter 1.

8 See *ex multis* Schabas and Murphy, *Research Handbook on International Courts and Tribunals*; Sarvarian, Baker, Fontanelli, and Tsevelekos, *Procedural Fairness in International Courts and Tribunals*; Giorgetti, *Challenges and Recusals of Judges and Arbitrators in International Courts and Tribunals*; Giorgetti, 'Between Legitimacy and Control: Challenges and Recusals of Judges and Arbitrators in International Courts and Tribunals', 205–258; Cohen, Follesdal, Grossman, and Ulfstein, *Legitimacy and International Courts*; de Chazournes, 'Plurality in the Fabric of International Courts and Tribunals: The Threads of a Managerial Approach', 13–72; Mégret, 'International Judges and Experts' Impartiality and the Problem of Past Declarations', 31–66 (2011).

9 Gómez, *Key Duties of International Investment Arbitrators*, *supra*, Chapter 1, note 1, 13.

10 UNCITRAL Rules on Transparency in Treaty-based Investor-State Arbitration, available at https://uncitral.un.org/sites/uncitral.un.org/files/media-documents/uncitral/en/rules-on-transparency-e.pdf. See generally Dimitrij Euler, Markus Gehring, Maxi Scherer (eds.), *Transparency in International Investment Arbitration – A Guide to the UNCITRAL Rules on Transparency in Treaty-Based Investor-State Arbitration*, Cambridge, 2015.

gathering together the various principles on the duties of arbitrators – as it has been the case with the aforementioned Code of Conduct for Arbitrators in International Investment Dispute Resolution.

In light of these considerations, this chapter will clarify the fundamental principles underpinning the duty of arbitrators. For the sake of brevity and practicality, the primary reference point will be the ICSID Convention and Arbitration Rules. Where necessary, these will be supplemented by the UNCITRAL Arbitration Rules,[11] relevant provisions from recent bilateral investment treaties (BITs) and free trade agreements (FTAs), the aforementioned IBA Guidelines on Conflicts of Interest in International Arbitration, and pertinent case law.

Article 14 of the ICSID Convention states that '[p]erson[s] [...] designated to serve on the panels shall be persons of high moral character and recognized competence in the fields of law, commerce, industry or finance, who may be relied upon to exercise independent judgment. Competence in the field of law shall be of particular importance in the case of persons on the Panel of Arbitrators'. Even though this provision is aimed at describing the characteristics of persons appointed to the Panel of Conciliators or the Panel of Arbitrators under Article 12 of the Convention, the norm in question also applies to anyone who is appointed to serve on an ICSID tribunal, as confirmed in Article 40(2).[12] The provision in Article 14 already underscores a number of duties of investment arbitrators, some of which are certainly measurable, while some others are less clear. Those who are appointed to an ICSID tribunal must be persons 'of high moral character', must be sufficiently educated to master at least one of the main aspects of the proceedings (be that the legal or one of the factual ones, although virtually every arbitrator appointed to an ICSID tribunal is a lawyer, as preferred by the drafters of the Convention), and be independent from the dispute.[13]

---

11 Available at https://uncitral.un.org/en/texts/arbitration/contractualtexts/arbitration.

12 'Arbitrators appointed from outside the Panel of Arbitrators shall possess the qualities stated in paragraph (1) of Article 14'.

13 It is interesting to note that, notwithstanding the emphasis on the importance of legal competence for persons on the Panel of Arbitrators, this provision does not render non-lawyers ineligible for inclusion on the Panel of Arbitrators or as members of an arbitral tribunal; however, the lack of qualified legal professionals on a tribunal may complicate the drafting of an award in compliance with Article 48 and could heighten the risk of annulment under Article 52(1). The lack of any of these qualities might also constitute grounds for disqualification of an arbitrator under Article 57 of the Convention. See Christoph H. Schreuer, Loretta Malintoppi, August Reinisch, Anthony Sinclair, *The ICSID Convention: a commentary*, *supra*, Chapter 1, note 21, 49.

Arbitrators are also under a duty to decide a dispute in accordance 'with such rules of law as may be agreed by the parties'. The same article 42(1) states that '[i]n the absence of such agreement, the Tribunal shall apply the law of the Contracting State party to the dispute [...] and such rules of international law as may be applicable'. It can therefore be argued that the principle *iura novit curia* applies to investment arbitrators, as well as the duty to know and understand at the proficiency level the applicable law, be that international law, a BIT, or a domestic law in certain cases.[14]

A rather peculiar duty is introduced in the ICSID Convention by Article 44. This provision will be addressed in greater detail in the remainder of this chapter;[15] however, a few words should be spent at this stage too. The provision in question states that 'if any question of procedure arises which is not covered by this Section or the Arbitration Rules or any rules agreed by the parties, the Tribunal shall decide the question'. This provision is usually discussed amongst the powers of the arbitral tribunals, and perhaps with good reason: not only because it is formally included in Section 3 of the Convention, named 'Powers and Functions of the Tribunal' but also because the terminology of the provision ('the Tribunal shall decide the question') seems to underscore the ability of the tribunal to transcend the applicable procedure rules and feel any gap in such rules with their own decision. However, the first part of Article 44 reiterates the importance of party autonomy even in investment arbitration.[16] Indeed, this provision states that the proceedings shall be conducted 'in accordance with the provisions of this Section and [...] in accordance with the arbitration rules in effect on the date on which the parties consented to arbitration', but it also affirms that the parties may agree otherwise. The fact that the procedure remains, not unlike in international commercial arbitration, in the hands of the parties, that

14 Müller, 'Iura Novit Curia versus Iura Novit Arbiter in International Arbitration', 137–142; Houtte, Maurizio Brunetti, 'Investment arbitration – ten areas of caution for commercial arbitrators', 553–574; and for a comparative perspective Carbone, 'Iura novit curia e arbitrato commerciale internazionale', 353–366.

15 See *infra*, Chapter 2.5.

16 James Devaney, 'Selecting Investment Arbitrators: Reconciling Party Autonomy and the International Rule of Law', KFG Working Paper Series, No. 33, Berlin Potsdam Research Group 'The International Rule of Law – Rise or Decline?', Berlin, May 2019, available at https://d-nb.info/1218169273/34; Jacob, 'Reinvigorating ICSID With a New Mission and With Renewed Respect for Party Autonomy', 123–160; Tanzi, 'On judicial autonomy and the autonomy of the parties in international adjudication, with special regard to investment arbitration and ICSID annulment proceedings', 57–75; Giorgetti, 'Who decides who decides in international investment arbitration', 431–486.

can amend, modify or replace procedure rules, suggests that the tribunal's power to decide procedural questions not covered by the applicable rules is to be exercised taking into account the applicable rules as chosen, expressly or implicitly by acceptance, by the parties; and any decision of the tribunal with regard to questions of procedure not covered by the applicable rules must be consistent with the rest of such applicable rules.

Other duties of investment arbitrators can be inferred from the declaration that each arbitrator appointed to an ICSID tribunal must sign. Under Arbitration Rule 6(2), arbitrators must keep any information learned during their participation to the proceedings as well as the content of the award confidential. They have a duty of fairness in deciding upon the claims, a duty (as already mentioned by the convention) to decide in accordance with the applicable law, and especially not to accept 'any instruction or compensation with regard to the proceeding from any source'.[17] Finally, arbitrators are under a duty of disclosure of their 'past and present professional, business, or other relationship with the parties, and 'any other circumstance that might cause [their] reliability for independent judgement to be questioned by a party'.

It is arguable, in light of the content of the ICSID Convention and the ICSID Arbitration Rules, that the main duties of investment arbitrators can be gathered into four main macro-categories: the duty to remain impartial and independent from the parties to the dispute at all times, the duty to apply the applicable law properly and fairly, a duty to remain up to date with regard to the international law on foreign investment and its most recent developments, and the duty to keep the proceedings, the award, and any information exchanged or delivered by the parties in the context of the proceedings confidential. Fach Gómez also identifies a duty of personal diligence and

17 Rule 6(2) is usually raised in the context of corruption on part of a member of the tribunal. Corruption can be defined as improper conduct by an arbitrator motivated by personal gain, and under Rule 6(2), it is evident if it can be demonstrated that biased behaviour resulted from improper 'compensation'. The acceptance of an improper payment in connection with ICSID proceedings would create a strong presumption of corruption, which is a ground for annulment under Article 52(1)(c). I have chosen not to address the issue of corruption in this book because, even though the duty of arbitrators to avoid corruption is undoubtedly significant, it lies beyond the scope of the current discussion: this book focuses on whether it is the responsibility of arbitrators to address the imbalance between investors and states in investment arbitration; the question of corruption pertains solely to the professional conduct of arbitrators and does not substantively impact the nature and scope of investment arbitral proceedings in the context of this analysis.

integrity, that would comprise the duty of non-delegation of responsibilities, time-related availability and appropriate behaviour.[18] However, I believe that such duties are already comprised in the four macro-categories previously identified: specifically, the duty of non-delegation of responsibilities and time-related availability fall within the duty of impartiality and independence as well as to fairly judge the dispute; and the duty to behave appropriately spreads over the four categories. It is also recognised by Fach Gómez that 'the duties discussed here cannot be treated as watertight compartments' as they are often somehow connected, and that 'they can therefore be placed at different points within the general framework of arbitrator's duties contained for instance in Codes of conduct, without undermining the overall charter of duties'.[19] Such duties of personal diligence and integrity, therefore, will be addressed as they become relevant in the next four subsections of this chapter.

2.2. Impartiality and Independence

Impartiality and independence are commonly considered as staples of international arbitration.[20] The very foundation of arbitration as a reliable alternative dispute resolution mechanism lies on the fact that arbitrators must possess some of the qualities normally required of domestic and international judges.[21] Of these qualities, impartiality and independence are of paramount significance. Arbitration is not merely an instrument to reach a settlement of a dispute between two parties: it is an instrument of administration of justice, first and foremost, and there cannot be justice if a member of the arbitral tribunal is not impartial as to the outcome of the dispute and independent from both parties (including the party that appointed them).[22] These two

18 Gómez, *Key Duties of International Investment Arbitrators*, *supra*, Chapter 1, note 1, 123.

19 *Ibid.*

20 See *supra*, Chapter 2, note 1.

21 The inquiry into the analogies and discrepancies between arbitrators and judges, both from a duty-related and a philosophical perspective, is undeniably intriguing. I briefly explore this topic in Chapter 4.4. For the sake of brevity, I direct the reader to the contributions to this debate of Chiara Giorgetti, *Challenges and recusals of judges and arbitrators in international courts and tribunals*, *supra*, Chapter 2, note 8; Gélinas, 'The Independence of International Arbitrators and Judges: Tampered with or Well Tempered?', 1–48; Nariman, 'Standards of Behaviour of Arbitrators', 311–321; Kaden, 'Judges and Arbitrators: Observations on the Scope of Judicial Review', 267–298.

22 See the interesting remarks of Mattli, 'Private justice in a global economy: from litigation to arbitration', 919–947; and Gross, 'Arbitration Archetypes for Enhancing Access to Justice', 2319–2336.

requirements are so significant that the drafters of the ICSID Convention, just like those of many other sets of arbitration rules, did not consider fundamental to include definitions of impartiality and independence – nor, in fact, to list both requirements explicitly.[23] As previously stated, Article 14 of the ICSID Convention requires arbitrators to be capable of decide independently on the matter at hand; and their necessary impartiality can be inferred as a requirement from the aforementioned text of ICSID Arbitration Rule 6(2).

It can be argued, however, that the ICSID Convention might in fact be one of the most explicit instruments in terms of providing some indication as to the extent of the requirements of impartiality and independence. By way of comparison, the UNCITRAL Arbitration Rules provide at Article 11 that any prospective arbitrator must disclose 'any circumstances likely to give rise to justifiable doubts as to his or her impartiality or independence', at Article 12 that '[a]ny arbitrator may be challenged if circumstances exist that give rise to justifiable doubts as to the arbitrator's impartiality or independence'.[24] However, no further definitions are provided for the terms impartiality and independence. This is also true for the ICC Arbitration Rules, which merely require that the statement submitted by appointed arbitrators 'contains no qualification regarding impartiality or independence or that a qualified statement regarding impartiality or independence has not given rise to objections'.[25] Similarly, the SCC Arbitration Rules simply state that 'every arbitrator must be impartial and independent' and that 'before being appointed, a prospective arbitrator shall disclose any circumstances that may give rise to justifiable doubts as to the prospective arbitrator's impartiality or independence'.[26]

---

23 It is somewhat puzzling, yet it contributes to the intriguing nature of international arbitration, that certain requirements are deemed so fundamental that their definitions are considered redundant and unnecessary. Consequently, most sets of arbitration rules do not deem it essential to define impartiality and independence explicitly or implicitly. On this lack of definitions may I refer the reader to Vargiu and Seatzu, 'Three Views of a Secret: Missed Opportunities in the ECHR's Recent Case-Law on International Commercial Arbitration', 1–21.

24 UNCITRAL Arbitration Rules (with article 1, paragraph 4, as adopted in 2013 and article 1, para. 5, as adopted in 2021), available at https://uncitral.un.org/sites/uncitral.un.org/files/media-documents/uncitral/en/21-07996_expedited-arbitration-e-ebook.pdf (last visited 15 November 2022).

25 International Chamber of Commerce, 2021 Rules of Arbitration, Art. 13(2), available at https://iccwbo.org/dispute-resolution-services/arbitration/rules-of-arbitration/ (last visited 15 November 2022).

26 Arbitration Institute of the Stockholm Chamber of Commerce, Arbitration Rules, Art. 18(1) and (2), available at https://sccarbitrationinstitute.se/wp-content/uploads/2024/12/SCC_Arbitration_Rules_2023_English.pdf (last visited 3 February 2025).

The LCIA Rules are somewhat more explicit, stipulating that 'all arbitrators shall be and remain at all times impartial and independent of the parties', that 'none shall act in the arbitration as advocate for or authorised representative of any party', and that 'no arbitrator shall give advice to any party on the parties' dispute or the conduct or outcome of the arbitration'.[27] Prospective appointees must also submit a declaration as to 'whether there are any circumstances currently known to the candidate which are likely to give rise in the mind of any party to any justifiable doubts as to his or her impartiality or independence and, if so, specifying in full such circumstances in the declaration'.[28] However, even the LCIA Rules treat partiality and lack of independence as matters of fact rather than law, emphasising the importance of perceived rather than actual bias. Interestingly, the arbitration rules of the ACR state in Article 6 that every arbitrator must be impartial and independent from the parties, while also requiring appointees to disclose 'any relationship with the parties or their counsel that may affect their independence and impartiality' and 'any personal or economic interest, direct or indirect, relating to the subject of the dispute'.

Even the IBA guidelines on Conflict of Interest in International Arbitration[29] are not entirely clear as to the precise meaning of the terms 'impartiality' and 'independence'. The general principle laid down in the guidelines merely states that '[e]very arbitrator shall be impartial and independent of the parties at the time of accepting an appointment to serve and shall remain so until the final award has been rendered or the proceedings have otherwise finally terminated'. Guideline 2 emphasises on the appearance and perception of bias, and states that an arbitrator must decline to accept an appointment or must resign from a tribunal in any case in which they have any doubt as to their ability to be impartial or independent; moreover, they should also step down 'if facts or circumstances exist, or have arisen since the appointment, which, from the point of view of a reasonable third person having knowledge of the relevant facts and circumstances, would give rise to justifiable doubts as to the arbitrator's impartiality or independence'.[30] The definition of justifiable doubt refers to the concept of 'reasonable third person', and relies on the fact that such reasonable third person, having knowledge of the relevant facts

27 The London Court of International Arbitration, Arbitration Rules 2020, Art. 5(3), available at https://www.lcia.org/media/download.aspx?MediaId=837 (last visited 15 November 2022).

28 *Ibid.*, Art. 5(4).

29 *Supra*, Chapter 2, note 6.

30 Guideline 2(b).

and circumstances, 'would reach the conclusion that there is a likelihood that the arbitrator may be influenced by factors other than the merits of the case as presented by the parties in reaching his or her decision'.[31] It is essential to highlight that this provision effectively offers a negative definition of impartiality and independence: specifically, it implies that an arbitrator is not considered impartial or independent if their decision is influenced by any factors other than the merits of the case. Such a negative definition would underscore the principle that arbitrators must remain free from external influences, biases, or personal interests that could compromise their judgment. Therefore, impartiality and independence are thereby defined by the absence of any doubt on undue influences or conflicts of interest that might sway the arbitrator's decision-making process. However, the nonwaivable read list in the guidelines comes to help in better understanding what sort of circumstances would raise such doubts. Such circumstances can be summarised as when there is a direct or indirect identity between a party and the arbitrator, when the arbitrator 'has a controlling influence on one of the parties or an entity that has a direct economic interest in the award to be rendered in the arbitration', when an arbitrator has a significant financial or personal interest in the outcome of the case or the activities of one of the parties, and, finally, when the arbitrator or their firm are regular advisors for one of the parties. In all these cases, even though there is no legal presumption that the arbitrator is not impartial or independent, there are grounds for justifiable doubts as to their relationships with the parties; therefore, should an arbitrator not decline the appointment or resign after the appointment, they might be subject to a challenge for disqualification. The IBA Guidelines also provide for a waivable red list – that is, a list of circumstances in which the impartiality or independence of the arbitrator is to be considered as doubtful, but the parties could waive their right to challenge nonetheless. The waivable red list is slightly longer, and includes situations in which the arbitrator has an existing relationship to the dispute, a direct or indirect interest in the dispute, or pre-existing relationships with the parties or the counsels. There are, moreover, the so-called orange list and green list, that, even though they do not necessarily put the independence

31 Guideline 2(c). Comparative perspectives are offered by Lee, 'Arbitrator's Evident Partiality: Current US Standards and Possible Solutions Based on Comparative Reviews', 159–176; Turunen, 'Arbitrators, Disclosure and Challenges: Are We Being Practical or Too Sensitive?', 371–392; Carrara, 'Conflicts of Interests', 379–396; Petti, Nathalie Voser, 'The Revised IBA Guidelines on Conflicts of Interest in International Arbitration', 6–36.

or impartiality of the arbitrator in question, require disclosure to the parties (who will be deemed to have accepted them shall they not immediately raise the issue) or may not even be disclosed as they do not pose a serious threat to the arbitrator's impartiality and independence. Indeed, the green list includes situations that are not uncommon in international arbitration, and especially in a relatively small circle like investment arbitration: examples of these situations are the previous expression of a legal opinion on an issue that also arises in the arbitration, or the fact that an arbitrator has a relationship with one of the counsels via membership to the same professional association or through a social media network.

In conclusion, a combined reading of the ICSID Convention and Arbitration Rules – or any of the aforementioned sets of arbitration rules commonly used in investment arbitration – and the IBA Guidelines on Conflict of Interest in International Arbitration allows to define impartiality and independence from the parties and the dispute as the lack of identity between and arbitrator and the parties to a dispute, the lack of controlling, financial, or personal interest in the dispute, and the lack of any direct relationship with the arbitrators firm or legal offices and one of the parties. More in general, arbitrators have a duty to abstain from being involved in any dispute in which they have not only any interest in the outcome but also any previous involvement – be that the provision of legal advice to one of the parties or a relationship with any person or company directly involved in the dispute.

2.3. The Applicable Law

The question of applicable law is not just one that concerns the choice made by the parties, or the various sources apply in an international investment arbiter proceedings. Indeed, it can be argued that the issue of applicable law is directly related to the responsibilities and duties of arbitrators. As previously stated, Article 42 of the ICSID Convention requires arbitral tribunals to decide upon the claims presented before them in accordance with the rules of law agreed upon by the parties, or the law of the host state should such agreement not exist.[32] In reality, most investment arbitral proceedings (both ICSID and *ad hoc*) are based not on an arbitration clause in a contract, but rather on a clause in a BIT or an FTA, by virtue of which the contracting states elect the jurisdiction of the ICSID or an *ad hoc* arbitral tribunal for any case that might arise between them and a national of another

32 See *supra*, Chapter 2.1.

contracting state.[33] Therefore, the agreement on the applicable law usually exists, whether expressly or impliedly, and it points to the BIT or FTA and the rules of domestic law that might be relevant depending on the party great investment. To this, Article 42 – and, in truth, the public international law nature of the dispute – adds 'such rules of international law as may be applicable'. Such provision is to be read in conjunction with Articles 52(1)(b) and (d) of the ICSID Convention, according to which an award might be annulled if, among others, a Tribunal has manifestly exceeded its powers or there has been a serious departure from a fundamental rule of procedure. The case-law of the ICSID shows that the wrongful application of the applicable law can be considered a manifest excess of powers, as is – even more often – the application of a law different from that implicitly or expressly chosen by the parties. As stated in *Helnan v. Egypt*, the notion of powers of the tribunal encompasses more than just its jurisdiction, and it includes the range of tasks assigned to the tribunal by the parties and the agreed-upon method for executing these tasks. Therefore, if the tribunal fails to apply the law selected by the parties (as opposed to merely misapplying it), it is deemed an overreach of its powers, a perspective acknowledged by both the Contracting States of the ICSID Convention and *ad hoc* committees. Additionally, if the tribunal fails to address a question entrusted to it, this too is considered an excess of powers, as it signifies a failure to execute the mandate given by the parties' agreement.[34] Similarly, the award in *Malaysian Historical Salvors v. Malaysia* was annulled because the tribunal incorrectly determined that there was no investment under the BIT, and consequently no jurisdiction: the tribunal concluded there was no investment under the ICSID Convention and did not assess whether an investment existed under the relevant BIT. Consequently,

---

33 On the expression of consent to investment arbitration see generally Radović, *Beyond Consent: Revisiting Jurisdiction in Investment Treaty Arbitration*; Shen, 'Is This a Great Leap Forward? A Comparative Review of the Investor-State Arbitration Clause in the ASEAN-China Investment Treaty: From BIT Jurisprudential and Practical Perspectives', 379–419; Tupa, *The Dilemma of Consent to International Arbitration in Investment Agreements without a Forum*; Potestà, 'The interpretation of consent to ICSID arbitration contained in domestic investment laws', 149–169; Tupa, 'Il consenso all'arbitrato ICSID contenuto in una legge nazionale dello stato ospite dell'investimento', 375–396; Fouret, 'Denunciation of the Washington Convention and Non-Contractual Investment Arbitration: "Manufacturing Consent" to ICSID Arbitration?', 71–87; Schreuer, 'Consent to Arbitration', 830.

34 Helnan International Hotels A/S v. Arab Republic of Egypt, ICSID Case No. ARB/05/19, Decision of the ad hoc Committee, 14 June 2010, para. 41. See also Timmer, 'Manifest Excess of Powers as a Ground for the Annulment of ICSID Awards', 775–803.

the *ad hoc* Committee found that 'the failure of the Sole Arbitrator even to consider, let alone apply, the definition of investment as it is contained in the [BIT] to be a gross error that gave rise to a manifest failure to exercise jurisdiction'.[35] The arbitrators have therefore a duty to apply the relevant applicable law and, to a certain extent, to apply it correctly.[36] It is also accepted that the concept of applicable law in investment arbitration encompasses customary international law, as clarified by the *ad hoc* Committee in *Enron v. Argentina*.[37] It is worth underscoring that the annulment Committee in *Amco Asia v. Indonesia* clarified that an *ad hoc* Committee must review the law applied by the Tribunal not to scrutinise whether the Tribunal made errors in interpreting the requirements of applicable law or in assessing the relevant facts to which the law was applied – as such scrutiny is the responsibility of a court of appeals – but solely to determining whether the Tribunal applied the law it was required to apply to the dispute. A failure to apply this law,

---

35 Malaysian Historical Salvors, SDN, BHD v. The Government of Malaysia, ICSID Case No. ARB/05/10, Decision on the Application for Annulment, 16 April 2009, para. 75. See also para. 61: '[B]y the terms of the [BIT], and for its purposes, the Contract is an investment. There is no room for another conclusion. The Sole Arbitrator did not reach another considered conclusion in respect of the Agreement. He rather chose to examine, virtually exclusively, the question of whether there was an investment within the meaning of Article 25(1) of the ICSID Convention. Finding that there was not, he found that 'it is unnecessary to discuss whether the Contract is an 'investment' under the BIT'.

36 The award in Vivendi v. Argentina was partially annulled because the tribunal neglected to apply the relevant BIT, focusing solely on the investors' claims under a concession contract: Compañiá de Aguas del Aconquija S.A. and Vivendi Universal S.A. v. Argentine Republic, ICSID Case No. ARB/97/3 (formerly Compañía de Aguas del Aconquija, S.A. and Compagnie Générale des Eaux v. Argentine Republic), Decision on Annulment, 3 July 2002, para. 108. See also Anzorena, 'Vivendi v. Argentina: on the Admissibility of Requests for Partial Annulment and the Ground of Manifest Excess of Powers', 123–175; Bernardini, 'Annulment of Awards', 168–188.

37 Enron Corporation and Ponderosa Assets, L.P. v. Argentine Republic, ICSID Case No. ARB/01/3, Decision on the Application for Annulment of the Argentine Republic, 30 July 2010, para. 377: 'The Tribunal was required to determine whether, on the proper construction of Article 25(1)(a) of the ILC Articles, the 'only way' requirement in that provision was satisfied, and not merely whether, from an economic perspective, there were other options available for dealing with the economic crisis. The Committee concludes that in determining that the measures adopted were not the 'only way', the Tribunal did not in fact apply Article 25(1)(a) of the ILC Articles (or more precisely, customary international law as reflected in that provision), but instead applied an expert opinion on an economic issue. In all the circumstances the Committee finds that this amounts to a failure to apply the applicable law, as ground of annulment under Article 52(1)(b) of the ICSID Convention.

as opposed to merely misconstruing it, would constitute a manifest excess of powers.[38] The line, however, is not always clear: as stated by the *ad hoc* Committee in *Soufraki v. UAE*, '[m]isinterpretation or misapplication of the proper law may, in particular cases, be so gross or egregious as substantially to amount to failure to apply the proper law. Such gross and consequential misinterpretation or misapplication of the proper law which no reasonable person (*'bon pere de famille'*) could accept needs to be distinguished from simple error – even a serious error – in the interpretation of the law which in many national jurisdictions may be the subject of ordinary appeal as distinguished from, e.g., an extraordinary writ of *certiorari*. In the present annulment proceedings, both Claimant and Respondent have acknowledged during the oral hearing that an egregiously wrong interpretation of the proper law – though nothing short of that – may amount to annullable error'.[39]

Moreover, the arbitrators cannot depart from fundamental rules of procedure.[40] Granted, the principle expressed in Article 44 allows the arbitrators a certain discretion with regard to filling any gaps in the procedural rules to be applied to the dispute; however, there is no room for ignoring the most important principles governing the procedure, and the case law has clearly shown that, should the arbitrators depart from a fundamental rule of procedure, the annulment of the award is the most likely outcome. This ground is indeed typically associated with issues of fairness, which are largely encompassed by the parties' right to present their case, their right to equal treatment,[41] and the necessity that the tribunal upholds fundamental principles

---

38 Amco Asia Corporation and others v. Republic of Indonesia, ICSID Case No. ARB/81/1, Ad hoc Committee Decision on the Application for Annulment, 16 May 1986, para. 23.

39 Hussein Nuaman Soufraki v. The United Arab Emirates, ICSID Case No. ARB/02/7, Decision of the ad hoc Committee on the Application for Annulment of Mr Soufraki, 5 June 2007, para. 86. See also Curzi, '"No matter how egregious": misapplication of the law and manifest excess of powers in ICSID arbitration', 303–323.

40 ICSID Convention, Article 51(1)(d).

41 The right to equal treatment, while raised multiple times, has been found violated only in the second annulment in Amco Asia v. Republic of Indonesia, *supra*, Chapter 2, note 38, Decision on the Applications for Annulment of the 1990 Award and the 1990 Supplemental Award, 17 December 1992, para. 9.08: 'The mandatory rule in question, Rule 49 (4), requiring a time limit to be fixed for the Parties to file their observations must be considered as fundamental. If a Tribunal takes a decision on the request of a Party without giving the other Party an opportunity to express itself on that request, it does not treat the Parties equally. In *MINE v. Guinea* [...], the Ad Hoc Committee considered the comparable provision of Article 18 of the UNCITRAL Model Law on International Commercial Arbitration as a clear example of a fundamental rule. This rule states:

of due process and natural justice. As clarified in *Wena Hotels v. Egypt*, a fundamental rule of procedure refers to a 'set of minimal standards of procedure to be respected as a matter of international law'.[42] In several cases, tribunals have been found to violate procedural fairness, impacting the outcome of their decisions. In *Amco Asia v. Indonesia II*, the tribunal applied a new framework of liability without notifying the parties, depriving them of the opportunity to address key issues that determined the case's outcome.[43] Similarly, in *Fraport v. Philippines*, the tribunal considered a prosecutor's resolution disclosed after the proceedings had concluded, which provided legal evidence on the legality of Fraport's investment under the law of the Philippines. The parties were not given a chance to respond to these findings, leading the *ad hoc* Committee to conclude that this evidence influenced the tribunal's reasoning on the Philippines' objection to the jurisdiction of the ICSID.[44] Furthermore, in *TECO v. Guatemala*, the tribunal denied interest on TECO's unjust enrichment claim without the issue being contested by the State or raised during arbitration, which was deemed a breach of procedural fairness.[45] Finally, in *Pey Casado v. Chile*, the *ad hoc* Committee found that Chile was not given an opportunity to present its defence and evidence regarding damages for an alleged breach of an investment treaty.[46] Interestingly, rules on the taking of evidence do not seem to pertain to the scope of application of Article 52(1)(d): both the annulment Committees in *Churchill Mining v. Indonesia* and *Continental Casualty v. Argentina*

'The parties shall be treated equally and each party shall be given full opportunity of presenting his case' [...] An argument could be made that in the case of rectification of an apparent clerical, arithmetical or similar error, there is hardly any need to fix a time limit for the Parties to file their observations. However, Rule 49 (4) expressly requires that the Tribunal fix a time limit in such cases. This rule of procedure does not lose its fundamental character by the fact that the decision to be taken might seem apparent'.

42 Wena Hotels Ltd. v. Arab Republic of Egypt, ICSID Case No. ARB/98/4, Decision on Annulment, 5 February 2002, para. 57.

43 Amco Asia v. Republic of Indonesia, *supra*, Chapter 2, note 38, Decision on the Applications for Annulment of the 1990 Award and the 1990 Supplemental Award, 17 December 1992, para. 5.22.

44 Fraport AG Frankfurt Airport Services v. Republic of the Philippines (I), ICSID Case No. ARB/03/25, Decision on Annulment, 23 December 2010, paras. 241–245.

45 TECO Guatemala Holdings LLC v Republic of Guatemala, ICSID Case No. ARB/10/23, Decision on Annulment, 5 April 2016, para. 183.

46 Victor Pey Casado and President Allende Foundation v Republic of Chile, ICSID Case No. ARB/98/2, Decision on the Application for Annulment of the Republic of Chile, 28 December 2012, para. 175.

stated that tribunals are not required to apply or explicitly state any particular burden or standard of proof.[47]

Finally, under Article 52(1)(e) of the ICSID Convention, there is a duty for arbitrators to state the reasons upon which the award is based. However, the Convention does not offer specific guidance on when a failure to provide reasons has occurred or how a tribunal's reasons should be articulated. Consequently, the central issue concerning Article 52(1)(e) is the standard of reasoning necessary to avoid annulment. The insufficiency or inadequacy of reasons is a notably subjective criterion, and *ad hoc* Committees have struggled with its precise application. The *MINE* case has become a foundational reference in the developing jurisprudence on this issue. The test established in *MINE v. Guinea* essentially requires that relevant reasons must exist and be understandable. According to the *ad hoc* Committee, the requirement to state reasons is met as long as the award allows one to follow the tribunal's reasoning 'from Point A to Point B' and ultimately to its conclusion, even if it contains errors of fact or law. This minimum requirement is particularly not met by reasons that are either contradictory or frivolous.[48] The *MINE* test, however, has been rejected by the *ad hoc* Committee in *Tidewater v. Venezuela*, in which it was noted that, to avoid evaluating the quality of the reasons, categorising 'frivolous' reasons as a subset of insufficient reasons under the MINE test was inappropriate. Instead, the relevant test, according to the Committee, was whether a reasonable reader of the award could understand the tribunal's

---

47 Churchill Mining PLC and Planet Mining Pty Ltd. v. Republic of Indonesia, ICSID Case No. ARB/12/14 and 12/40, Decision on Annulment, 18 March 2019, para. 214; Continental Casualty Company v. The Argentine Republic, ICSID Case No. ARB/03/9, Decision on the Application for Partial Annulment, and the Application for Partial Annulment, 16 September 2011, para. 135: 'The Committee notes that the ICSID Convention and the Arbitration Rules contain no provisions with respect to the burden of proof or standard of proof. Accordingly, there cannot be any requirement that a tribunal expressly apply a particular burden of proof or standard of proof in determining the dispute before it. Indeed, the tribunal is not obliged expressly to articulate any specific burden of proof or standard of proof and to analyse the evidence in those terms, as opposed simply to making findings of fact on the basis of the evidence before it'.

48 Maritime International Nominees Establishment v. Republic of Guinea, ICSID Case No. ARB/84/4, Decision of the *ad hoc* Annulment Committee, 22 December 1989, paras. 5.08 and 5.09: 'the requirement that an award has to be motivated implies that it must enable the reader to follow the reasoning of the Tribunal on points of fact and law. It implies that, and only that. The adequacy of the reasoning is not an appropriate standard of review under paragraph (1)(e), because it almost inevitably draws an *ad hoc* Committee into an examination of the substance of the tribunal's decision, in disregard of the exclusion of the remedy of appeal by Article 53 of the Convention'.

reasoning.[49] Obviously, in order to properly apply the relevant laws, rules and procedures to the disputes, the arbitrators must be familiar with such laws, as well as the norms of public international law on foreign investment. This, in turn, creates a duty of knowledge and awareness of the law.

2.4. Knowledge and Expertise

As it has been seen in the previous section, the question of applicable law in international arbitration is one upon which much ink has been spilled. In fact, the scholarly debate is so vibrant and prolific that even to attempt a short literature review would be quite a rather trying – and probably unnecessary in this context – task.[50] In terms of duties of the arbitrators, in fact, the question of applicable law is specifically relevant for one aspect – that is, the fact that arbitrators are subject to a specific duty to apply the law chosen by the parties. However, unlike in international commercial arbitration, a context where the parties choose and applicable law or such law is identified through rather specific criteria pointing towards one or more domestic laws,[51] in investment arbitration the question of applicable law is made a complicated by the public international law nature of proceedings in which one of the parties is a private entity – and there is usually a contract between such entity and the host state, in addition to the treaty protecting the said entity as national of another contracting state.

49 Tidewater Inc., Tidewater Investment SRL, Tidewater Caribe, C.A., et al. v. The Bolivarian Republic of Venezuela, ICSID Case No. ARB/10/5, Decision on Annulment, 27 December 2016, para. 129.

50 See *ex multis* Cordero-Moss and Fernández Arroyo, *Applicable Law Issues in International Arbitration*, *supra*, Chapter 2, note 39; Nozari, *Applicable Law in International Arbitration: The Experience of ICSID and Iran-United States Claims Tribunal*; Loizou, *Establishing the Content of the Applicable Law in International Arbitration*; Kjos, *Applicable Law in Investor-State Arbitration: The Interplay between National and International Law*, *supra*, Chapter 1, note 5; Crook, 'Applicable Law in International Arbitration: The Iran-U.S. Claims Tribunal Experience', 278–311; Zarra, 'Applicable Law in Investment Arbitration: the 2021 Practice', *supra* note 5, Chapter 1, note 5; Wahab, 'Ascertaining the Content of the Applicable Law in International Arbitration: Converging Civil and Common Law Approaches', 412–422.

51 Cordero-Moss *International Commercial Contracts: Contract Terms, Applicable Law and Arbitration*; Moses, *The Principles and Practice of International Commercial Arbitration*; Smit and Pěchota, *International Commercial Arbitration and the Courts*; Cîrlig, 'The arbitral tribunal's authority to determine the applicable law in international commercial arbitration: patterns and trends', 18–32; and the seminal Born, *International Commercial Arbitration* 2817–3000.

As previously mentioned, Article 42(1) of the ICSID Convention states that '[t]he Tribunal shall decide a dispute in accordance with such rules of law as may be agreed by the parties'. This provision mirrors those in most other arbitral instruments that also underscore the primacy of the principle of party autonomy: the UNCITRAL Arbitration Rules state that '[t]he arbitral tribunal shall apply the rules of law designated by the parties as applicable to the substance of the dispute';[52] similarly, the International Chamber of Commerce (ICC) Arbitration Rules provide that '[t]he parties shall be free to agree upon the rules of law to be applied by the arbitral tribunal to the merits of the dispute',[53] while the Stockholm Chamber of Commerce (SCC) Arbitration Rules include a provision according to which '[t]he Arbitral Tribunal shall decide the merits of the dispute on the basis of the law(s) or rules of law agreed upon by the parties'.[54] The recent Vienna International Arbitral Centre Rules of Investment Arbitration, too, provide that '[t]he arbitral tribunal shall decide the dispute in accordance with the law or rules of law agreed upon by the parties'.[55] It could be argued, therefore, that Article 42 of the ICSID Convention is finely modelled upon the tradition of international commercial arbitration. However, the practice of international investment arbitration shows that in most cases, there is actually no choice of law provision in the BITs upon which the arbitral proceedings are based.[56] Moreover, those treaties that do contain a choice of law clause of some sort, usually provide for the provisions of the treaty itself as the law according to which the dispute is to be resolved. Otherwise, the identification of the applicable law depends

---

52 United Nations Commission on International Trade Law Arbitration Rules, adopted in 1976, as revised in 2010 and 2013 (the UNCITRAL Arbitration Rules), Article 35(1).

53 Rules of Arbitration of the International Chamber of Commerce, adopted in 2012, as amended in 2017 and 2021 (the ICC Arbitration Rules), Article 21(1).

54 Arbitration Rules of the Arbitration Institute of the Stockholm Chamber of Commerce, adopted in 2017 (the SCC Arbitration Rules), Article 27(1).

55 Rules of Investment Arbitration of the Vienna International Arbitral Centre (the Vienna Investment Arbitration Rules), Article 27(1).

56 See Antonio Parra, 'Applicable Law in Investor-State Arbitration', in Michael Rovine, *Contemporary Issues in International Arbitration and Mediation: The Fordham Papers*, Vol. I, Martinus Nijhoff, 2008, pp. 3, 7–8, where he noted that, as of 19 June 2007, 15 out of 20 ICSID awards decided on the merits under bilateral investment treaties did not contain a choice of law provision. The other five treaties specified that the applicable law included the treaty itself, general principles of international law, and the law of the host State. See also Gaillard and Banifatemi, 'The Meaning of "and" in Article 42 (1), Second Sentence, of the Washington Convention: The Role of International Law in the ICSID Choice of Law Process', 375–411; Schwebel, 'A BIT about ICSID', 1–9; Schreuer, 'Jurisdiction and Applicable Law in Investment Treaty Arbitration', 1–25.

on the arbitration rules chosen by the parties to conduct the proceedings. However, it is necessary to remember that the underlying treaty has a rather specific role in investment arbitration; it is because of this role that the BIT is usually considered the main source of applicable law, even in those cases in which there is neither an explicit choice of law clause nor a provision pointing to the BIT itself as applicable law. Therefore, it can be said that the BIT is the chief instrument for the regulation of the relationship between the investor and the host state. The BIT is an instrument of international law, and therefore, any gaps or matters that are not regulated by the treaty are to be addressed according to customary international law, as well as any other treaty in force between the host state and the state of nationality of the investor. This is confirmed by the aforementioned Article 42(1) of the ICSID Convention, which points out that the applicable rules of international law are to be taken into consideration regardless of whether there is an express choice of law by the parties, or the law of the host state is applied due to the lack of such choice.

This raises the question as to the extent to which arbitrators must know the applicable law. As stated in ICSID Arbitration Rule 6, when an arbitrator is appointed they must declare that they shall judge between the parties according to the applicable law. The declaration under Rule 6, however, does not capture the full picture of the arbitrator's task. First, arbitral tribunals must rule on their own jurisdiction; ICSID tribunals must do so according to what is prescribed by Article 25(1) and especially Article 41 of the ICSID Convention,[57] whilst other tribunals would judge on their own jurisdiction based on the *competence de la competence* principle.[58] Additionally, the merits of the case must be decided according to the proper applicable law, and it is crucial that such law be applied properly. It is worth reiterating that the mechanisms available for reviewing arbitral awards within the framework

57 Article 41 of the ICSID Convention explicitly states that '(1) The Tribunal shall be the judge of its own competence. (2) Any objection by a party to the dispute that that dispute is not within the jurisdiction of the Centre, or for other reasons is not within the competence of the Tribunal, shall be considered by the Tribunal'.

58 Kröll and Keller, 'The Competence-Competence Principle's Positive Effect', *supra*, Chapter 1, note 3, 771–806; Barceló III, 'The Competence-Competence Principle's Negative Effect', Kröll and Keller, 807–847; Amerasinghe, *International Arbitral Jurisdiction*, 21–46; Samuel, 'The US Supreme Court does Kompetenz-Kompetenz', 263–273; Landolt, 'The Inconvenience of Principle: Separability and Kompetenz-Kompetenz', 511–530; Visconte, 'Competência Arbitral. Princípio Kompetenz-Kompetenz. Alegação de Contrato de Adesão', 93–109; Park, 'The Arbitrability Dicta in *First Options v. Kaplan*: What Sort of Kompetenz-Kompetenz Has Crossed the Atlantic?', 137–160.

of investment arbitration are notably constrained. These limitations predominantly concern the merits of the cases heard by the arbitral tribunals, avoiding a thorough examination of the substantive correctness of the arbitral decisions.[59] The dichotomy between procedural integrity and substantive correctness is fundamental to understanding the limitations of review mechanisms in investment arbitration. Procedural integrity pertains to the adherence to rules and principles governing the arbitral proceedings. This includes ensuring fairness, transparency, and impartiality in the conduct of proceedings, on top of respecting the rules on the establishment of the tribunal, the conduct of the arbitrators *vis-à-vis* the parties, the application of the relevant laws, and the content and motivation of the award. In contrast, substantive correctness involves the accurate application and interpretation of the relevant laws and facts to reach a just decision on the merits of the case. Current review mechanisms, as previously mentioned, primarily focus on procedural integrity. Under the ICSID Convention, annulment proceedings are limited to specific grounds such as the improper constitution of the tribunal, corruption of an arbitrator, a serious departure from a fundamental rule of procedure, the tribunal's manifest excess of powers, or a failure to state the reasons on which the award is based. These grounds do not encompass a review of the substantive correctness of the arbitral award, as they are

59 Article 53(1) famously states that '[t]he award shall be binding on the parties and shall not be subject to any appeal or to any other remedy except those provided for in this Convention. Each party shall abide by and comply with the terms of the award except to the extent that enforcement shall have been stayed pursuant to the relevant provisions of this Convention'. Critics have traditionally argued that the absence of an appellate mechanism can result in the enforcement of flawed awards, undermining fairness and consistency in investment arbitration, and that an appeal process is necessary to ensure greater accuracy and legitimacy in arbitral rulings, aligning ICSID procedures with those of other judicial systems. See generally Nilsson and Englesson, 'Inconsistent Awards in Investment Treaty Arbitration: Is an Appeals Court Needed?', 561–579; Caron, 'Reputation and Reality in the ICSID Annulment Process: Understanding the Distinction Between Annulment and Appeal', 21–56; Knull and Robins, 'Betting the Farm on International Arbitration: Is It Time to Offer an Appeal Option?' 531–577; Goldhaber, 'Wanted: a World Investment Court'; Legum, 'Options to establish an Appellate Mechanism for Investment Disputes', in Karl Sauvant, *Appeals Mechanism in International Investment Disputes* 231–240; McRae, 'The WTO Appellate Body: A Model for an ICSID Appeals Facility?', 371–387; Qureshi, 'An appellate system in international investment arbitration?', *supra*, Chapter 2, note 33, 1154; Schreuer, 'ICSID Annulment Revisited', 103–122; Tams, 'An Appealing Option? The Debate about an ICSID Appellate Structure', 14; Walsh, 'Substantive Review of ICSID Awards: Is the Desire for Accuracy Sufficient to Compromise Finality?', 444–462.

fundamentally procedural in nature.[60] As such, even if an arbitral tribunal misinterprets or misapplies the law, resulting in an incorrect decision, the award remains largely insulated from annulment on these grounds.

In non-ICSID cases, review mechanisms are generally governed by the domestic arbitration laws of the seat of arbitration or the seat of enforcement. These laws vary significantly across jurisdictions but commonly provide for limited judicial review of arbitral awards. For example, the UNCITRAL Model Law on International Commercial Arbitration, adopted or incorporated in some form by many a jurisdiction, allows for setting aside an award on grounds similar to those under the ICSID Convention, such as the incapacity of a party, the invalidity of the arbitration agreement, the lack of proper notice or inability to present the case, an excess of authority by the tribunal, the improper composition of the tribunal or the failure to respect the procedural rules chosen by the parties, and conflicts with the public policy of the seat of arbitration or the seat of enforcement.[61] These grounds too, like those in Article 52(1) of the ICSID Convention, are primarily procedural and do not extend towards a review of the substantive merits of the award. Judicial intervention by the seat of enforcement is therefore rather limited outside of the ICSID context too; this on one hand reinforces the finality of arbitral awards and the autonomy of the arbitral process from the constraints and possible conflicts of interest with domestic jurisdictions, although on the other hand it does so at the expense of potentially upholding substantively incorrect decisions.

This limited scope of review in investment arbitration has obvious and profound implications on decision-making and the development of international investment law. The core elements of correct decision-making in investment arbitration, just as in court proceedings, could be distilled into the accurate identification and precise application of the applicable law. However, the review mechanisms currently available to dissatisfied parties do not adequately

60 See *supra*, Chapter 2.3.

61 UNCITRAL Model Law on International Commercial Arbitration 1985, with amendments as adopted in 2006, available at https://uncitral.un.org/sites/uncitral.un.org/files/media-documents/uncitral/en/19-09955_e_ebook.pdf, Article 34. See Pietro Ortolani, 'Article 34: Application for Setting Aside as Exclusive Recourse against Arbitral Award', in Bantekas, Ortolani, Ali, Gomez, and Polkinghorne, *UNCITRAL Model Law on International Commercial Arbitration: A Commentary* 858–898; Cuniberti, *The UNCITRAL Model Law on International Commercial Arbitration: A Commentary*; Hill, 'Claims that an arbitral tribunal failed to deal with an issue: the setting aside of awards under the Arbitration Act 1996 and the UNCITRAL Model Law on International Commercial Arbitration', 385–414; Tan and Hwang, 'The Time Limit to Set Aside an Award Under Article 34(3) of the Model Law: A Comparative Study', 553–600.

safeguard against substantive errors. These limitations have contributed to the legitimacy crisis of investment arbitration, as stakeholders perceive arbitral awards as lacking rigorous oversight.[62] Furthermore, the emphasis on procedural integrity over substantive correctness may lead to situations where incorrect legal interpretations remain unchallenged. This can not only create inconsistencies in the application of international investment law, potentially affecting the predictability and reliability of the whole dispute settlement system and the confidence that many stakeholders have in the mechanism, but also normalise debatable interpretations of rules of investment law.[63]

While questionable, this element of potential inconsistency is not a peculiarity of international investment law. Public international law is characterised by the absence of a compulsory formalised third-party mechanism for determining the correctness of judicial decisions. Unlike domestic legal systems, where appellate courts or similar entities are mandated to review and correct judicial decisions, international law operates without such hierarchical oversight. This structural feature stems from the sovereignty of states and the consensual nature of international legal obligations. In international investment law, consent to arbitration is expressed in arbitration clauses in BITs and rarely challenged unless the host state believes that the claim filed by the investor is not covered by the scope of application of the relevant BIT.[64] The awards issued by arbitral tribunals are final and binding, with limited scope for annulment. This situation contrasts

---

62 A partial bibliography on the legitimacy crisis of investment arbitration can be found *supra*, Chapter 1, note 3.

63 See for instance the debate on the extension of BIT clauses on the Most Favoured Nation treatment standard to procedural rights, efficiently portrayed by Sharmin and Laryea, 'Application of MFN to investment dispute settlement: rule of law issues', 21–41; Waibel, 'Putting the MFN Genie Back in the Bottle', 60–63; Douglas, 'The MFN Clause in Investment Arbitration: Treaty Interpretation Off the Rails', 97–113; Junngam, 'An MFN Clause and BIT Dispute Settlement: a Host State's Implied Consent to Arbitration by Reference', 399–528. From a more general standpoint, see Sun, 'A New Test Toward Consistency in International Investment Arbitration', 121–138.

64 Siwy, 'Contract Claims and Treaty Claims', 209–255; Alexandrov, 'Breach of Treaty Claims and Breach of Contract Claims: when can an International Tribunal exercise Jurisdiction?', 370–394; Alexandrov, 'Breach of Treaty Claims and Breach of Contract Claims: is it still Unknown Territory?', Alexandrov, 323–350; Demirkol, 'Non-treaty Claims in Investment Treaty Arbitration', 59–91; Shany, 'Contract Claims vs. Treaty Claims: Mapping Conflicts between ICSID Decisions on Multisourced Investment Claims', 835–851; Schreuer, 'Investment Treaty Arbitration and Jurisdiction over Contract Claims: the Vivendi I Case considered', 281–323; Ren, 'The Dichotomy between Jurisdiction and Admissibility in International Arbitration', 417–446.

sharply with domestic legal systems, where a structured appellate process ensures greater coherence and uniformity in legal interpretation. As stated beforehand, the absence of a formalised third-party review mechanism in public international law can be attributed to the fundamental principles of state sovereignty and the consensual nature of international adjudication. This decentralised approach, while respecting state sovereignty, inevitably leads to a fragmented legal landscape where different tribunals may interpret international law divergently. The issue is further complicated in international investment law, where the interests of states and private investors must be balanced, and where different arbitral tribunals may interpret similar – when not identical – provision differently within the very same system. Investors seek predictability and protection for their investments, while states aim to preserve their regulatory autonomy.[65] The current system, lacking a compulsory review mechanism, struggles to provide the level of certainty and consistency desired by the parties.[66]

In numerous instances, ICSID *ad hoc* Committees have determined that a tribunal had manifestly exceeded its powers by making incorrect jurisdictional findings. This includes situations where tribunals have exercised jurisdiction that did not in fact exist,[67] exceeded their

---

65 See Hafner-Burton, Steinert-Threlkeld, Victor, 'Predictability Versus Flexibility: Secrecy in International Investment Arbitration', 413–453; Schultz and Dupont, 'Investment arbitration: Promoting the rule of law or over-empowering investors?: A quantitative empirical study', 1147–1168; Gotanda, 'Consistently Inconsistent: The Need for Predictability in Awarding Costs and Fees in Investment Treaty Arbitrations', 420–437; Chen, 'Precedent and dialogue in investment treaty arbitration', *supra*, Chapter 1, note 18; and in contrast Schultz, 'Against consistency in investment arbitration', 297–316.

66 This is also one of the reasons why there have been calls for the establishment of an appellate mechanism in international investment arbitration to address these deficiencies. Such a mechanism could certainly enhance the coherence of international investment law by providing a consistent interpretative authority; the creation of such a body, however, has faced significant political and practical challenges, including the need for widespread state consent and the potential for increased costs and delays in dispute resolution – a debate summarized *supra*, Chapter 2, note 59.

67 Mr. Patrick Mitchell v. Democratic Republic of the Congo, ICSID Case No. ARB/99/7, Decision on the Application for Annulment of the Award, 1 November 2006, paras. 47–48: 'The *ad hoc* Committee is thus inclined to believe that the Arbitral Tribunal forced the concept of investment in the case at hand in order to affirm its jurisdiction. This is perhaps attributable to the discomfort engendered in the Arbitral Tribunal by the factual circumstances of the case, namely the violent dispossession of the Claimant's property and good will. The fact remains, however, that this combination of flaws in the Award is such that an excess of power on the part of the Arbitral Tribunal must be acknowledged'.

jurisdiction[68] or rejected jurisdiction that did exist.[69] These errors highlight the issues inherent in the determination of the jurisdiction of investment arbitral tribunals. Jurisdictional issues are crucial as they determine the scope and authority of the tribunal to hear a case, and incorrect jurisdictional findings can lead to substantial injustices and undermine the legitimacy of the arbitration process. However, it is not solely the procedural missteps but also substantive errors in interpreting the scope of jurisdictional provisions that lead to such findings. The role of *ad hoc* Committees is critical in this context, as they provide a mechanism to address these jurisdictional errors. However, their findings on correctness are case-specific (at least in theory) and apply only to the disputing parties involved. Consequently, the conclusions of one ICSID *ad hoc* Committee may be subsequently rejected by other arbitral tribunals or even by other ICSID *ad hoc* committees, with all the problematic consequences that this would lead to in terms of coherency of the system and overall perception of legitimacy and reliability.

Outside of the ICSID context, the domestic courts of the seat of enforcement can review international arbitral tribunals' decisions according to the law of the seat of the arbitration as well as their own.[70] These reviews typically provide for some level of scrutiny of jurisdictional findings, although the stringency of such reviews varies across jurisdictions. Courts in various countries, including Canada, the Netherlands, Singapore, Sweden, Switzerland and the United Kingdom, have set aside arbitral awards due to incorrect jurisdictional findings.[71] However, generalising the practices of

---

68 Occidental Petroleum Corporation and Occidental Exploration and Production Company v. The Republic of Ecuador, ICSID Case No. ARB/06/11, Decision on Annulment of the Award, 2 November 2015, para. 266: 'By compensating a protected investor for an investment which is beneficially owned by a non-protected investor, the Tribunal has illicitly expanded the scope of its jurisdiction and has acted with an excess of powers'.

69 Malaysian Historical Salvors v. Malaysia, *supra*, Chapter 2, note 35; Helnan v. Egypt, *supra*, Chapter 2, note 34.

70 United Nations, Convention on the Recognition and Enforcement of Foreign Arbitral Awards, 10 June 1958, United Nations Treaty Series, vol. 330, p. 3. See generally Kronke, Nacimiento, Otto and Christine Port, *Recognition and Enforcement of Foreign Arbitral Awards: A Global Commentary on the New York Convention* 205–344; Fons and Alonso, 'The New York Convention and the Enforcement of Arbitration Agreements by National Courts: What Level of Review?'.

71 For reasons of conciseness may I refer the reader to Rowley and Siino, *The Guide to Challenging and Enforcing Arbitration Awards*, GAR – Law Business Research, 2023, also available at https://globalarbitrationreview.com/guide/the-guide-challenging-and-enforcing-arbitration-awards/3rd-edition; and the recent Hanno Wehland,

domestic courts in this context is challenging due to the limited number of cases, the unique nature of the issues addressed, and the differences in the application of domestic arbitration laws.[72] The incorrectness of investment awards on substantive matters, as stated beforehand, rarely falls within the express mandate of existing review mechanisms: even a 'manifestly incorrect application of the law' is not a ground for annulment under the ICSID Convention. It is evident that there has traditionally been a broader reluctance within international arbitration to engage in substantive review of arbitral decisions, prioritising finality and efficiency over correctness.

Another indirect way of challenging the correctness of investment decisions on substantive matters under ICSID annulment procedures is by invoking the annulment ground under Article 52(1)(e), which concerns the failure of an award to state the reasons on which it is based. ICSID annulment committees have set aside several awards on this basis, either partially or fully.[73] However, the correctness or persuasiveness of the reasoning is not relevant under Article 52(1)(e). A majority of *ad hoc* committees have concluded that 'frivolous' and 'contradictory' reasons are equivalent to no reasons and could justify annulment. This ground for annulment underscores the importance of reasoned awards in ensuring the transparency and accountability of arbitral tribunals, even though it does not directly address substantive correctness.

A further few words should be spent on the issue of misapplication of applicable law in the context of international investment arbitration, which is evidently a critical concern that can undermine the legitimacy and effectiveness of arbitral awards. This misapplication can manifest in several ways. One of the primary forms of misapplication of law in international arbitration is the excessively broad or narrow interpretation of legal

---

'Setting-Aside Proceedings Against Treaty- Based Arbitral Awards in Switzerland and Their Contribution to the Debate Regarding the Fundamental Requirements for Protection under Investment Treaties', 559–576.

72 Even in states that have adopted the UNCITRAL Model Law on International Commercial Arbitration, or have modelled their own arbitration laws upon it, domestic legal culture, traditions, and customs often result in differing and sometimes diverging interpretations of otherwise similar legal principles. These variations occur because local judicial practices, historical legal frameworks, and cultural attitudes towards arbitration influence how the Model Law's provisions are understood and applied. Consequently, despite a common legislative foundation, the implementation and interpretation of arbitration laws can vary significantly from one jurisdiction to another, affecting the consistency and predictability of international arbitration outcomes.

73 See *supra*, Chapter 2.3.

obligations.[74] When tribunals interpret legal provisions too broadly, they may extend obligations beyond the intentions of the parties or the explicit mandate of the relevant treaty. Conversely, overly narrow interpretations can unduly restrict the scope of protections or obligations envisaged by the legal framework. An excessively broad interpretation can also occur, when tribunals impose obligations or grant rights that extend beyond the reasonable expectations of the parties. This issue is particularly pertinent in the context of investment treaties, which often contain broad and general language intended to provide a framework for investment protection rather than detailed prescriptions. For example, the Fair and Equitable Treatment standard, commonly found in investment treaties, aims to ensure a stable and predictable investment environment.[75] However, some tribunals have interpreted this standard so broadly that it effectively imposes on host states obligations akin to a comprehensive insurance policy against all forms of adverse regulatory change.[76] Such interpretations can deter states from enacting necessary regulatory measures due to fear of potential arbitral claims, thus infringing on their sovereign right to regulate in the public interest. On the other hand, an overly narrow interpretation can undermine the protective purposes of investment treaties. Tribunals may interpret key provisions in a manner that severely limits their applicability, thereby depriving investors of the protections that the treaties were intended to afford. For instance, a narrow interpretation of indirect expropriation

74 An exemplary instance is the decision of the *ad hoc* Committee in Occidental Petroleum v. Ecuador, *supra*, Chapter 2, note 68.

75 From the extensive body of scholarship on the fair and equitable treatment standard I would like to refer the attention of the reader to a few volumes, such as Paparinskis, *The International Minimum Standard and Fair and Equitable Treatment* 111–153; Živković, *Fair and Equitable Treatment and the Rule of Law*; Palombino, *Fair and Equitable Treatment and the Fabric of General principles*; Kläger, '*Fair and Equitable Treatment*' *in International Investment Law*; Islam, *The Fair and Equitable Treatment (FET) Standard in International Investment Arbitration: Developing Countries in Context*; Diehl, *The Core Standard of International Investment Protection: Fair and Equitable Treatment*; Tudor, *The Fair and Equitable Treatment Standard in the International Law of Foreign Investment.*

76 See e.g. Waste Management, Inc. v. United Mexican States, ICSID Case No. ARB(AF)/00/3, Award, April 30, 2004, para. 98; Pope & Talbot Inc. v. The Government of Canada, UNCITRAL, Award on the Merits of Phase 2, 10 April 2001, paras. 105–118. See also UNCTAD, *World Investment Report 2012: Towards a New Generation of Investment Policies*, available at http://www.unctad-docs.org/files/UNCTAD-WIR2012-Full-en.pdf, para. 139; Monti and Fermeglia, 'The FET Standard between Treaty Reform and ISDS Practice: An Analysis of the Modernized ECT', 155–178.

clauses may fail to recognise legitimate instances where regulatory actions, though non-discriminatory and in the public interest, substantially diminish the value of an investment. By setting an unduly high threshold for what constitutes indirect expropriation, tribunals can effectively deny investors the protection they reasonably expected under the treaty.[77]

Even though each arbitral award is only binding upon its parties, the nature of investment arbitration as a system, or at least as a regime, is hardly questionable[78]; therefore, problematic awards, even when issued against third states, may lead to adverse policy outcomes: overly stringent interpretations of investment protections might encourage regulatory chill, where states refrain from enacting beneficial regulations due to fear of arbitration claims.[79] This can be particularly detrimental in areas requiring proactive regulation, such as environmental protection and public health. Similarly, impractical standards set by tribunals might lead to excessive litigation, with investors frequently challenging regulatory measures.

---

77 Indirect expropriation refers to actions by a state that do not directly seize property but effectively deprive the owner of the use, benefit, or value of the property. It is challenging to identify because it involves subtle and nuanced interferences, such as regulatory measures or administrative actions, that do not involve outright transfer of ownership. The difficulty lies in distinguishing between legitimate state regulation in the public interest and actions that unfairly target-specific investments, thereby indirectly expropriating them. Determining whether such actions constitute indirect expropriation requires a careful analysis of the intent, impact, and proportionality of the state measures involved. On narrow interpretations of the concept of indirect expropriation see in particular Dani and Akhtar-Khavari, 'The Uncertainty of Legal Doctrine in Indirect Expropriation Cases and the Legitimacy Problems of Investment Arbitration', 1–32; Nanteuil, 'Expropriation', 127–157; Isakoff, 'Defining the Scope of Indirect Expropriation for International Investments', 189–210; Riffel, 'Indirect Expropriation and the Protection of Public Interests', 945–974.

78 On the definition of the system of investment law as a regime and the significance of such semantic choice see the groundbreaking volume by Bonnitcha, Poulsen, and Waibel, *The Political Economy of the Investment Treaty Regime*, See also Kulick, *Reassertion of Control over the Investment Treaty Regime*; Sauvant and Alvarez, *The Evolving International Investment Regime: Expectations, Realities, Options.*

79 See for instance Vytiaganets, 'Smoking Chills? Tobacco Regulatory Chill, Foreign Investment, and the NCD Crisis in the Post-Soviet Case: a Case Study from Ukraine', 753–780; Tienhaara, 'Regulatory chill in a warming world: The threat to climate policy posed by Investor-State Dispute Settlement', 229–250; Berge and Berger, 'Do Investor-State Dispute Settlement Cases Influence Domestic Environmental Regulation? The Role of Respondent State Bureaucratic Capacity', 1–41; Janeba, 'Regulatory chill and the effect of investor state dispute settlements', 1172–1198; Hagemann, 'The North-South Divide of Regulatory Chill: A Comparative Analysis of the Impact of Investor-State Dispute Settlement on Policy Makers in Developed and Developing Countries', 27–48.

2.5. Confidentiality

The level of confidentiality in investment arbitral proceedings is significantly influenced by the agreements made between the parties involved and the applicable provisions under which the arbitration is conducted. This framework means that the extent to which case details are kept confidential can vary widely depending on the specific agreements made. If the parties do not agree on the confidentiality terms, arbitral tribunals established under the ICSID Convention have the authority to determine the level of confidentiality. For instance, in *Noble Ventures v. Romania*, the Tribunal determined that the ICSID Convention and the Arbitration Rules did not support the application of national discovery rules, and encouraged the parties to agree on document disclosure while considering specific factors highlighted by the Tribunal, particularly acknowledging that the Respondent was from a civil law jurisdiction where document production is less common than in common law countries. The Tribunal noted that ordering the production of documents could aid in establishing the facts pertinent to the case. However, it also acknowledged that the discovery process might be time-consuming, overly burdensome and potentially oppressive, with the burden possibly being disproportionate to the benefit. Additionally, the Tribunal recognised that parties might have legitimate confidentiality concerns.[80] However, ICSID tribunals have generally disfavoured claims of confidentiality by host states based on the confidential or politically sensitive nature of certain documents: in *Biwater Gauff v. Tanzania*, the Tribunal held in fact that issues related to document production can be resolved without adhering to national standards, as international tribunals are not obligated to follow national rules of evidence.[81]

---

80 Noble Ventures, Inc. v. Romania, ICSID Case No. ARB/01/11, Award, 12 October 2005, para. 20.

81 Biwater Gauff (Tanzania) Ltd. v. United Republic of Tanzania, ICSID Case No. ARB/05/22, Procedural Order No. 2, 24 May 2006, p. 8: '[t]he Arbitral Tribunal notes that the Respondent's identification of, and articulation of, 'public interest immunity' as a doctrine rests upon the national law of Tanzania [...] The Respondent notes that similar doctrines are accepted in other national legal systems. However, and importantly, no equivalent doctrine has been identified as a matter of public international law, or as part of the ICSID regime. Moreover, article 54(5) prohibits inquiries by 'any court', a term which is defined in the Tanzanian Constitution as any court having jurisdiction in the Republic of Tanzania. It may therefore be argued that this particular prohibition, by its own terms, does not apply to an ICSID Arbitral Tribunal. More fundamentally, however, the nature of this dispute resolution process is entirely different from a national court process. This is an international tribunal, governed by an international convention, which is mandated to enquire into the conduct and responsibility of a State in light of its international treaty and customary

When parties enter into an ICSID arbitration, they have the option to stipulate the confidentiality terms in their agreements. These agreements can cover a range of aspects, including whether hearings will be public or private, whether documents will be disclosed, and to whom information can be revealed. If the parties fail to specify these terms, the tribunal must refer to the governing investment treaty or other applicable legal documents to make a determination. In instances where the parties have not reached an agreement and applicable legal texts do not provide clear guidance, the tribunal has the responsibility to set the confidentiality standards.[82] This approach ensures that there is always a mechanism in place to protect the sensitive information that may be involved in such disputes.

Confidentiality in the ICSID system is further structured by specific rules within the Arbitration Rules. Rule 6(2) of these rules specifically addresses the confidentiality obligations of arbitrators, as it requires each arbitrator to sign a declaration affirming their commitment to confidentiality before or during the first session of the tribunal. This declaration is broad in scope, covering all information that the arbitrator gains access to as a result of their involvement in the proceedings, as well as the contents of any awards made by the tribunal. The wording of Rule 6(2) underscores the importance of confidentiality in maintaining the integrity and impartiality of the arbitration process. By means of committing to keep all information confidential, arbitrators help ensure that the parties can engage in the process without fear that their sensitive information will be disclosed. Additionally, Rule 15 of the Arbitration Rules mandates that the tribunal's deliberations be conducted in private and that these deliberations remain secret. This rule further reinforces the confidentiality of the arbitration process. Private deliberations help maintain the impartiality of the tribunal by preventing external influences and pressures. Keeping these deliberations secret ensures that the decision-making process is not subject to public scrutiny or interference, which could undermine the tribunal's effectiveness. For example, in *Loewen v. United States*, the Tribunal operating under the Additional

international law obligations. It is hardly conceivable that, in this setting, a State might invoke domestic notions of public interest and policy relating to the operations of its own Government as a basis to object to the production of documents which are relevant to determine whether the State has violated its international obligations and whether, therefore, its international responsibility is engaged'.

82 Knahr and Reinisch, 'Transparency versus Confidentiality in International Investment Arbitration – The Biwater Gauff Compromise', 97–118; Schreuer, Malintoppi, Reinisch, and Sinclair, *The ICSID Convention: A Commentary*, *supra*, Chapter 1, note 20, 698; Bělohlávek, 'Confidentiality and Publicity in Investment Arbitration, Public Interest and Scope of Powers Vested in Arbitral Tribunals', 23–45.

Facility was faced with a request from the United States to make all pleadings and minutes of the proceedings public. The Rules stipulated that minutes could not be published without the consent of both parties, and the Tribunal made its decision accordingly. At the same time, the Tribunal rejected the Claimant's assertion that there was a general obligation of confidentiality, but concluded nonetheless that public discussion during the proceedings should be restricted to what is necessary.[83]

Together, Rules 6(2) and 15 create a robust framework for ensuring confidentiality in ICSID arbitrations. These rules not only protect the sensitive information of the parties but also preserve the integrity and impartiality of the arbitration process, and provide clear guidelines that arbitrators should follow, thereby establishing a consistent standard of confidentiality across different cases. The broad confidentiality obligations imposed by these rules reflect the understanding that the information involved in investment disputes can be highly sensitive. This sensitivity can pertain to business strategies, financial data and other proprietary information that parties may not want to be disclosed publicly. By ensuring that such information remains confidential, the ICSID system helps maintain trust in the arbitration as a mechanism. In practice, the degree of confidentiality in ICSID cases can vary significantly. This variability is largely due to the diverse nature of investment treaties and other rules and principles that govern these disputes. The tribunal's role in setting confidentiality standards when there is no agreement between the parties or clear guidance from applicable rules is therefore critical. Arbitrators must balance the need for confidentiality with the principles of transparency and accountability. While confidentiality protects sensitive information, transparency in certain aspects of the process can enhance public trust and understanding of international investment arbitration. Moreover, the approach to confidentiality in ICSID arbitrations has evolved over time. There has been a growing recognition of the importance of transparency in international arbitration, particularly, in cases involving public interest issues. This trend has led to increased calls for the publication of awards and other documents in certain cases, subject to redaction of sensitive information.[84]

---

83 Loewen Group, Inc. and Raymond L. Loewen v. United States of America, ICSID Case No. ARB(AF)/98/3, Decision on Jurisdiction, 9 January 2001, para. 26.

84 See in particular Menaker and Hellbeck, 'Piercing the Veil of Confidentiality: the Recent Trend towards Greater Public Participation and Transparency in Investment Treaty Arbitration', *supra*, Chapter 2, note 64, 183–219; Jahodníková and Mičinský, 'Crossing the Rubicon – on the Correlation of the Principle of Transparency and Confidentiality of Arbitral Proceedings within the Area of International Investment Arbitration: Does Investment Arbitration have the Credentials to trump the Principle of Confidentiality in Arbitration?', 239–261.

The duty of confidentiality in international arbitration often intersects with the prohibition of *ex parte* communications. This principle mandates that arbitrators must not engage in private discussions with one party without the other party being present. This prohibition helps maintain the integrity and impartiality of the arbitration process by ensuring that all parties have equal access to the tribunal and its members. A notable illustration of this issue can be found in *Pey Casado v. Chile.*[85] In this instance, a party-appointed arbitrator was found to have communicated with his appointing party about the content of a partial award draft proposed by the president of the arbitral tribunal. This breach of confidentiality and the prohibition of *ex parte* communications led to the resignation of the arbitrator from the case. This incident underscores the critical importance of adhering to confidentiality rules to prevent any undue influence or bias in the arbitration process.[86] Another significant dimension of the duty of confidentiality in arbitration is its application concerning the arbitral institution itself. This was highlighted in the *Vivendi* case, in which, a member of the second *ad hoc* Committee issued an additional opinion emphasising the importance of maintaining the privacy and secrecy of the tribunal's deliberations and drafts, in line with Arbitration Rule 15. Jan Hendrik Dalhuisen indeed argued that the ICSID Secretariat might have been overstepping its original mandate and questioned whether the Secretariat was adhering to the duty of confidentiality as required.[87]

Notwithstanding these principles contained in Rules 6 and 15 of the ICSID Arbitration Rules, the application of confidentiality in arbitration can nonetheless be problematic and sometimes contentious. Different jurisdictions may have varying interpretations of confidentiality obligations, and thus arbitrators may interpret the scope and purposes of their duty of confidentiality differently. Moreover, the increasing push for transparency in international arbitration, driven by public interest considerations, has added another

85 Casado and President Allende Foundation v Republic of Chile, ICSID Case No. ARB/98/2, Award of 8 May 2008. See also Christoph. Schreuer, 'Víctor Pey Casado and President Allende Foundation v Republic of Chile: Barely an Annulment', 321–327.

86 Pey Casado v Chile, Award, 8 May 2008, paras. 34–43.

87 Compañía de Aguas del Aconquija S.A. and Vivendi Universal S.A. v. Argentine Republic, ICSID Case No. ARB/97/3, Decision on the Argentine Republic's Request for Annulment of the Award, 20 August 2007, Additional Opinion of Professor JH Dalhuisen under Article 48(4) of the ICSID Convention, para. 2: 'It is clear that the Secretariat wants to obtain for itself a greater role in the conduct of ICSID cases and in the process also wants to involve itself in the drafting of the decisions. So also in this case. I believe this in general to be outside the Secretariat's remit and undesirable'.

layer of complexity. Transparency advocates argue that greater openness in arbitration can enhance accountability and public trust, particularly, in cases involving states or public entities. Balancing confidentiality and transparency is a delicate task. Some arbitration institutions and recent treaties have sought to address this balance by introducing provisions that allow for the publication of awards and other documents, while still protecting sensitive information. These provisions often include mechanisms for redacting confidential information or allowing parties to object to the disclosure of certain documents. This approach aims to provide greater transparency while still respecting the confidentiality needs of the parties involved.

Until recently, the NAFTA Code of Conduct for Dispute Settlement Procedures under Chapters 19 and 20 established the primary guidelines for confidentiality obligations for investment arbitrators.[88] This Code clearly stated that '[a] member or former member shall not at any time disclose or use any non-public information concerning the proceeding or acquired during the proceeding except for the purposes of the proceeding and shall not, in any case, disclose or use any such information to gain personal advantage or advantage for others or to affect adversely the interest of another'.[89] This stringent directive ensured that arbitrators maintained a high level of confidentiality, protecting the integrity of the arbitration process and preventing any misuse of sensitive information, and effectively prohibited arbitrators from divulging or exploiting non-public details of the proceedings for personal gain or to benefit others, emphasising the importance of impartiality and fairness. Building on the foundations laid by the NAFTA Code, the recent Article 8 of the recent UNCITRAL Code of Conduct for Arbitrators in International Investment Dispute Resolution has taken these principles further, with detailed and comprehensive guidelines.[90] The text states that unless permitted by the instrument of consent, the applicable rules or agreement of the disputing parties, a Candidate, an Arbitrator or a former Arbitrator shall not disclose or use any information concerning, or acquired in connection with, the proceedings, or disclose any draft decision in the proceedings;[91] moreover, an Arbitrator or a former Arbitrator may comment on a decision rendered in a proceeding only if it was made publicly available

88 Code of Conduct for Dispute Settlement Procedures under Chapters 19 and 20 of the North American Free Trade Agreement, available at https://www.worldtradelaw.net/document.php?id=nafta/19-20code.pdf.

89 *Ibid.*, Rule VI(A).

90 *Supra*, Chapter 2, note 3.

91 *Ibid.*, Article 8(1).

in accordance with the instrument of consent or the applicable rules.[92] This provision broadens the scope of confidentiality to cover any information concerning the proceedings, not just non-public information, as it includes specific prohibitions on disclosing draft decisions, thereby reinforcing the privacy of the arbitration process at all stages.

Further stipulations under Article 8 enhance the protective measures surrounding the confidentiality of the arbitration process. The rule states that an arbitrator or a former arbitrator shall not disclose the contents of the deliberations in the proceedings, ensuring that the internal discussions and considerations of the tribunal remain private. This provision maintains the sanctity of the deliberation process, preventing external influences and preserving the neutrality of the tribunal's decision-making. Moreover, as stated beforehand, the Code allows arbitrators to comment on decisions only if they have been made publicly available in accordance with the instrument of consent or applicable rules. Even then, comments are restricted, especially when the proceedings are still pending or subject to post-award remedies or reviews. This careful regulation of commentary aims to prevent any undermining of the arbitration process' integrity. The rule against commenting while proceedings are ongoing or decisions are under review ensures that the arbitration process is not influenced or disrupted by premature public discussions.

Article 8 also addresses scenarios where arbitrators might be legally compelled to disclose information. The provision in question states that confidentiality obligations do not apply if a candidate, arbitrator or former arbitrator is legally required to disclose information in a court or other competent body, or needs to disclose information to protect or pursue legal rights. For example, an arbitrator may need to disclose confidential details in response to a subpoena issued by a domestic court. This exception ensures that arbitrators can comply with legal requirements without violating the Code's confidentiality rules.[93] The prohibition on disclosing or using information 'concerning, or acquired during, the proceedings' is thorough. The term 'disclose' refers to the unauthorised sharing or circulation of information, making it available to anyone who should not have access. The term 'use' refers to exploiting such information outside the proceedings, potentially to gain an advantage. This broad definition helps safeguard all sensitive information related to the arbitration.

Furthermore, the UNCITRAL Code of Conduct specifies that its confidentiality provisions do not prevent arbitrators from using information

92 *Ibid.*, Article 8(3).

93 *Ibid.*, Article 8(5).

for the purposes of the proceedings. Arbitrators are allowed to discuss information provided by the disputing parties among themselves to carry out their duties. This flexibility ensures that the tribunal can function effectively while maintaining confidentiality. Additionally, arbitrators can disclose basic information about proceedings in which they were involved, as required by other articles of the Code. The exception provided in paragraph 1 allows for the disclosure or use of information if permitted by the instrument of consent, applicable rules, or agreement of the disputing parties. For instance, an arbitrator might share a draft award with the disputing parties or the arbitral institution for feedback, if this is permitted by the applicable rules. However, this exception does not extend to the contents of deliberations, which must remain confidential.

Paragraph 3 of Article 8 clarifies that arbitrators can only comment on decisions that have been made publicly available in accordance with the instrument of consent or applicable rules. This means that arbitrators cannot comment on decisions that were improperly disclosed. Furthermore, even when commenting on publicly available decisions, arbitrators must not reveal the contents of deliberations or discuss why the tribunal reached a particular decision. This restriction helps protect the confidentiality of the deliberation process and ensures that the tribunal's internal decision-making is not subject to external scrutiny. While paragraph 3 allows for academic discussions of publicly available decisions, it emphasises that such comments must not undermine the integrity of the proceedings or the independence and impartiality of the arbitrators. Arbitrators are expected to maintain a high standard of professionalism in their public comments, avoiding any statements that could be interpreted as questioning the tribunal's decisions or processes.

Paragraph 4 further restricts the ability to comment on decisions by prohibiting comments while the proceedings are still pending or the decision is subject to post-award remedies or review. This ensures that the arbitration process is not compromised by premature public discussions. The term 'post-award remedy' includes processes like interpretation, correction or revision of the award, as well as annulment processes. The term 'review' refers to efforts to set aside the award or challenges to its enforcement. These restrictions are crucial to maintaining the fairness and impartiality of the arbitration process.

2.6. Powers *ex* Article 44 ICSID

Arbitral proceedings are generally governed by the specific rules and agreed upon by the parties involved. These rules are set to ensure the process is fair, transparent and consistent. According to Article 44 of the ICSID

Convention, '[a]ny arbitration proceeding shall be conducted in accordance with the provisions of this Section and, except as the parties otherwise agree, in accordance with the Arbitration Rules in effect on the date on which the parties consented to arbitration. If any question of procedure arises which is not covered by this Section or the Arbitration Rules or any rules agreed by the parties, the Tribunal shall decide the question'. The second sentence of the provision in question is particularly relevant for the duties of arbitrators, as it addresses situations where procedural questions arise that are not explicitly covered by the ICSID Convention, the arbitration rules agreed upon or any rules set by the parties. Article 44 of the ICSID states that, in such cases, the tribunal has the authority to decide on the procedural question, providing a mechanism for resolving unforeseen issues and ensures the arbitration process can proceed smoothly even when unexpected procedural questions arise.[94]

The flexibility provided by Article 44 is essential for several reasons. First, arbitration can involve complex disputes with unique circumstances that may not be fully anticipated by the pre-existing rules; by granting the tribunal the authority to decide on procedural questions not covered by the existing rules, the provision allows for the necessary adaptability to address these unique aspects of a dispute. This should ensure that the arbitral proceedings remain effective and efficient, avoiding unnecessary delays caused by procedural uncertainties. Second, this authority empowers the tribunal to tailor the procedural aspects of the arbitration to the specific needs of the case, and emphasises the importance of the tribunal's role in maintaining order and consistency in the arbitration process. Empowering the tribunal to resolve procedural questions, the provision helps ensure that the arbitration process remains within the bounds of the agreed-upon rules while also providing a clear path forward when those rules do not address a particular issue. Furthermore, one may argue that Article 44 implicitly encourages the parties to anticipate and agree upon as many procedural rules as possible before the arbitration begins. By doing so, the parties can minimise the number of

94 A full overview of these powers has been compiled by Jeffery Commission, Moloo, *Procedural Issues in International Investment Arbitration*. See also Manukyan, 'Hidden in the curtain of Article 44: Formation rules of arbitration agreements and ICSID arbitration rules', 67–85; Kabra, 'Has Abaclat v Argentina left the ICSID with a massive problem?', 425–453; Cordero-Moss, 'Tribunal's Power versus Party Autonomy', *supra*, Chapter 2, note 33, 1207; Woolhouse, 'Transparency and Procedural Integrity of Arbitration – The Biwater Tribunal's Balancing Act', Transnational Dispute Management 5 (2006), available at http://www.transnational-dispute-management.com/article.asp?key=825; and recently Torterola and Sharipov, 'The 2022 ICSID Arbitration Rules: Modernizing International Investment Dispute Resolution', 52–60.

procedural questions that the tribunal must decide, thus retaining greater control over the arbitration process. However, the provision also provides a safety net, ensuring that any procedural gaps left by the parties' agreements can be addressed by the tribunal. This, obviously, configures a duty upon the arbitrators not only to fill the gaps in the ICSID Convention and Rules, but to also do so in a manner consistent with such rules.

In practice, indeed, the tribunal's authority to decide on procedural questions can encompass a wide range of issues. These may include decisions on deadlines for submissions, the admissibility of certain types of evidence, the scheduling of hearings and the procedures for witness testimony, among others. The tribunal's ability to make these decisions ensures that the arbitration can adapt to the specific needs of the case and the parties, providing a more tailored and effective dispute resolution process. The tribunal's decisions on procedural matters must also be guided by the overarching principles of the arbitration rules and the intentions of the parties. Moreover, the provision ensures that the arbitration process does not come to a standstill due to procedural ambiguities. The provision in question, by granting the tribunal the authority to resolve procedural questions, prevents potential deadlocks that could arise from disagreements over procedural issues; and while these powers may be more pertaining to the role of international commercial arbitral tribunals, the variety of issues arising in the investment case-law suggest that the scope of Article 44 of the ICSID Convention should not be underestimated: in fact, it may be considered one of the most prominent duties of investment arbitrators, given the extensive scope of the provision (and, therefore, the extensive responsibility deriving from it). Moreover, Article 44, by establishing a wide array of duties without explicitly mentioning any, works perfectly as a bridging provision between the express duties of investment arbitrators, and the implied duties that shall be addressed in Chapter 3.

Chapter 3

ARBITRATORS BEYOND THEIR DISPUTES

In Chapter 2, the duties of investment arbitrators as outlined in the ICSID Convention and commonly adopted arbitration rules, along with the newly introduced UNCITRAL Code of Conduct for Arbitrators in International Investment Dispute Resolution,[1] were examined in detail. This analysis provided an overview of the explicit responsibilities of arbitrators in investment disputes. However, there exists a notion that beyond these explicit duties, there are additional implied obligations (also referred to in this chapter as 'implied duties') that investment arbitrators are expected to fulfil. These implicit duties, though not formally codified, are crucial to the effective functioning of arbitrators within the disputes they adjudicate and the broader context of international investment law. This chapter is aimed at identifying such duties and assess their significance in the system.

Some of these implied duties may be considered simply as collateral to the explicit ones: for instance, arbitrators are expected to conduct proceedings with a level of decorum and professionalism that reinforces the integrity of the arbitration process.[2] This includes treating all parties with respect and avoiding any behaviour that could be construed as prejudicial. The manner in which arbitrators manage hearings, their interactions with parties, and their overall demeanour can significantly influence perceptions of fairness and justice in the proceedings and arbitration as a dispute settlement mechanism. Furthermore, part of their duty to apply the relevant laws properly requires investment arbitrators to stay abreast of developments in

---

1 *Supra*, Chapter 2, note 4.

2 See generally the insights of Gaillard, 'Sociology of international arbitration', 1–17; Rogers, 'The Vocation of the International Arbitrator', 957–1020; Puig, 'Social capital in the arbitration market', 387–424; Kapeliuk, 'The repeat appointment factor: exploring decision patterns of elite investment arbitrators', 47–90; Giorgetti, 'Who decides who decides in international investment arbitration', *supra*, Chapter 2, note 16; Franck, Aaken, Freda, Guthrie, and Rachlinski, 'Inside the Arbitrator's Mind', 1115–1174.

international investment law and related fields.[3] After decades of relative immobility, international investment law has actually become quite dynamic, with frequent changes in treaties, regulations, and case-law.[4] Arbitrators must continuously update their knowledge and understanding of these developments to ensure that their decisions are informed and relevant. This requires a commitment to ongoing education and professional development, engaging with the case-law as well as contemporary legal scholarship. By fulfilling this implicit duty, arbitrators can make decisions that are not only legally sound but also reflect the current state of international investment law. Additionally, as it will be seen in this chapter, one may argue that there exists an implied duty of arbitrators to consider the broader implications of their decisions due to the *de facto* multilateral nature of the system of investment law.[5] Investment arbitration often involves questions of law and business that can have significant economic, political and social consequences. Arbitrators must be mindful of the potential impact of their decisions on the parties involved, as well as on the host state's regulatory environment and the international investment community at large. This requires a balanced approach that considers not only the legal merits of the case but also the broader context in which the dispute arises. By doing so, arbitrators can contribute to the development of a fair and stable international investment

3 As evidenced in Article 14(1) of the ICSID Convention, where it is explicitly stated that '[p]ersons designated to serve on the Panels shall be persons of [...] recognized competence in the fields of law, commerce, industry or finance' and that [c]ompetence in the field of law shall be of particular importance in the case of persons on the Panel of Arbitrators'. It is therefore essential that prospective arbitrators remain up-to-date with legal developments, maintaining current knowledge in the field and ensuring that they can effectively and accurately interpret and apply the law. See on this point Smith, 'Contractual obligations Owed by and to arbitrators: Model terms of Appointment', 17–40.

4 It is clearly reported in the ICSID website (https://icsid.worldbank.org/news-and-events/blogs/spotlight-icsid-caseload-statistics) that 'the figures were fairly low from the early 70s to the mid 90s – on average about two new cases a year. The case numbers started to climb in the late 90s and 2000s: first to around 10 new cases, then 20, and up to the current average of 35 to 50 cases filed per year, which is where the numbers have stabilized over the last 10 years or so'.

5 As theorized by Schill, *The Multilateralization of International Investment Law*, 365–367: 'the more recent failures of direct multilateralism in international investment relations do not contradict the suggestion that a general interest exists among States in having uniform investment rules and principles of investment protection [...] Investor-State arbitration as a compliance mechanism therefore contributes to understanding international investment law as an objective order that provides stable institutions for the functioning of a global market economy'. See also Salacuse, 'The emerging global regime for investment', 427–473.

regime that balances the interests of investors and host states. Furthermore, it has been argued, in various form, that arbitrators are under an implied duty of arbitrators to engage in ethical decision-making. Ethical considerations often play a crucial role in investment arbitration, particularly in cases involving issues such as human rights, environmental protection and social justice. According to these positions, arbitrators must be guided by ethical principles in their decision-making process, ensuring that their awards are not only legally sound but also morally justifiable. This involves a consideration of the ethical implications of their decisions and a commitment to upholding the highest standards of integrity and justice.[6] Lastly, investment arbitrators have a *de facto* duty to contribute to the development of international investment law. This duty, too, involves a commitment to legal scholarship and the development of jurisprudence that enhances the coherence and predictability of the legal framework governing international investment.[7]

3.1. Interpretation

A primary and paramount responsibility of investment arbitrators is the duty of interpretation. In Chapter 2, it has been established that arbitrators are expected to possess a thorough understanding of the applicable law and to interpret it accurately in pursuit of a just resolution of disputes, as a by-product of the provision in Article 42 of the ICSID Convention. However, the interpretive role of arbitrators frequently extends beyond the confines of simple interpretation and evolves into an actual law-making function, particularly when dealing with treaty law provisions that are ambiguously formulated or susceptible to multiple interpretations.[8] In such instances, arbitrators are not merely applying the law as it stands but are effectively shaping the legal

---

6 But see Dimsey and Pramod, 'Selection, Bias, and Ethics of Arbitrators in Investor-State Arbitration', 1–40; and da Silva Martins, 'Challenges to Transparency and Ethics in Alternatives to Arbitration in the Realm of International Investments', 321–376.

7 Vargiu, 'Stakeholders of Investment Arbitration: establishing a dialogue among arbitrators, states, investors, academics and other actors in international investment law', *supra*, Chapter 1, note 1; Franck, 'The role of international arbitrators', 499–522.

8 Sweet, Chung, and Saltzman, 'Arbitral lawmaking and state power: An empirical analysis of investor–state arbitration', 579–609; Bentolila, *Arbitrators as lawmakers, supra*, Chapter 1, note 1; and especially Titi, 'The arbitrator as a lawmaker: Jurisgenerative processes in investment arbitration', 829–851, who points out at p. 833 that '[r] emarkably, investment treaties are often laconic instruments that remain silent on a number of issues, leaving gaps that adjudicating tribunals are thus called to fill in. This is particularly true of old generation investment treaties, including the quasi-totality of bilateral investment treaties (BITs) concluded by EU Member States'.

landscape by clarifying (and sometimes outright creating)[9] norms that fill the gaps or resolve ambiguities in existing treaties and other instruments. This *quasi*-legislative (or jurisgenerative, as theorised by Titi)[10] function is especially pronounced in international investment law, where treaties often contain broadly phrased principles that require detailed interpretation to be effectively applied to specific cases. Through their awards, arbitrators contribute to the development of international legal standards, setting *de facto* precedents, or a *jurisprudence constante*, that influence future disputes as well as the behaviour of states and investors alike.[11] This interpretative duty thus

9 Salini Costruttori S.p.A. and Italstrade S.p.A. v. Kingdom of Morocco [I], ICSID Case No. ARB/00/4, *supra*, Chapter 1, note 20; Vargiu, '*Langue* and *Parole* of Investment Law', *supra*, Chapter 1, note 19, 305.

10 Titi, 'The arbitrator as a lawmaker: Jurisgenerative processes in investment arbitration', *supra*, Chapter 3, note 8, 830.

11 The concept of a 'common legal opinion or jurisprudence constante' was initially introduced by the Tribunal in SGS Société Générale de Surveillance S.A. v. Republic of the Philippines, ICSID Case No. ARB/02/6, Decision of the Tribunal on Objections to Jurisdiction, 29 January 2004, para. 97. The concept was then endorsed by the Tribunal in AES Corporation v. The Argentine Republic, ICSID Case No. ARB/02/17, Decision on Jurisdiction, 26 April 2005, para. 33: '[f]rom a more general point of view, one can hardly deny that the institutional dimension of the control mechanisms provided for under the ICSID Convention might well be a factor, in the longer term, for contributing to the development of a common legal opinion or *jurisprudence constante*, to resolve some difficult legal issues discussed in many cases, inasmuch as these issues share the same substantial features'. A similar approach was proposed by the Tribunal in ADC Affiliate Limited and ADC & ADMC Management Limited v. The Republic of Hungary, ICSID Case No. ARB/03/16, Award of the Tribunal, 2 October 2006, para. 293: '[i]t is true that arbitral awards do not constitute binding precedent. It is also true that a number of cases are fact-driven and that the findings in those cases cannot be transposed in and of themselves to other cases. It is further true that a number of cases are based on treaties that differ from the present BIT in certain respects. However, cautious reliance on certain principles developed in a number of those cases, as persuasive authority, may advance the body of law, which in turn may serve predictability in the interest of both investors and host States'. See *ex multis* Schill, *The Multilateralization of International Investment Law*, *supra*, Chapter 3, note 5, 338; Reed, 'The "De Facto" Precedent Regime in Investment Arbitration: a Case for Proactive Case Management', *supra*, Chapter 1, note 19; Vargiu, 'Langue and Parole of Investment Law', *supra*, Chapter 1, note 19, 300; Douglas, 'Can a doctrine of precedent be justified in investment treaty arbitration?', 104–110; Martinez-Fraga and Samra, 'The Role of Precedent in Defining Res Judicata in Investor – State Arbitration', 419–450; Kaufmann-Kohler, 'Arbitral Precedent: Dream, Necessity or Excuse – The 2006 Freshfields Lecture', 357–378; Brabandere, 'Arbitral Decisions As a Source of International Investment Law', 245–288; Ridi, 'Approaches to External Precedent: The Invocation of International Jurisprudence in Investment Arbitration and WTO Dispute Settlement', 121–148.

entails a significant responsibility, as arbitrators must balance the need for consistency and predictability in the application of law with the necessity to adapt legal principles to the different realities of each case.[12] Consequently, the interpretive function of arbitrators is not a mere passive task of uncovering the intentions of treaty drafters (as the Vienna Convention on the Law of Treaties would in fact indicate) but an active process of shaping the contours of international investment law. It is important to underscore that, alongside paragraph 1 ('[s] treaty shall be interpreted in good faith in accordance with the ordinary meaning to be given to the terms of the treaty in their context and in the light of its object and purpose'), Article 31 of the Vienna Convention states at paragraph 2 that '[t]he context for the purpose of the interpretation of a treaty shall comprise, in addition to the text, including its preamble and annexes: (a) any agreement relating to the treaty which was made between all the parties in connection with the conclusion of the treaty; (b) any instrument which was made by one or more parties in connection with the conclusion of the treaty and accepted by the other parties as an instrument related to the treaty'.[13] Not only, therefore, the ordinary meaning of the terms of an investment treaty in context must be given priority, but the reference in the Vienna Convention to other agreements signed by the parties as well as any other instruments 'accepted by the other parties as an instrument related to the treaty' may entail that arbitrators should consider that '[c]ross-treaty interpretation suggests that bilateral investment treaties (BITs), even though constituting bilateral treaties, yield to common rationales and refer to common concepts of international investment law that exist independent from the individual bilateral treaty relationships'.[14] Schill also notes that '[c]ross-treaty interpretation comes in two forms: reference to the BIT practice

12 Writing about the question of predictability in investment arbitration is rather challenging. Predictability in investment arbitration is desirable as it ensures consistency, fairness and reliability in dispute resolution, fostering confidence among investors and states alike. However, its importance may be ultimately overestimated because the unique and complex nature of each case often necessitates tailored decisions that deviate from established *de facto* precedents. Despite this, the concern remains significant, as a lack of predictability can lead to uncertainty and reduced trust in the arbitration system, potentially deterring investment and complicating international economic relations. Therefore, while striving for predictability is important, it something that arbitrator must balance with the need for flexibility and contextual decision-making.

13 United Nations, Vienna Convention on the Law of Treaties, United Nations, Treaty Series, vol. 1155, p. 331, 23 May 1969.

14 Schill, *The Multilateralization of International Investment Law*, *supra*, Chapter 3, note 5, 305.

of the States involved in a dispute and reference to the BIT practice of wholly unrelated third countries'; the states' acceptance of such practices seems to justify the opinion that states indeed consider BITs signed by third parties as related to their own investment agreements.[15]

Moreover, paragraph 3 of the same Article 31 of the Vienna Convention states that '[t]here shall be taken into account, together with the context: (a) any subsequent agreement between the parties regarding the interpretation of the treaty or the application of its provisions; (b) any subsequent practice in the application of the treaty which establishes the agreement of the parties regarding its interpretation; (c) any relevant rules of international law applicable in the relations between the parties'. This seems to further strengthen the idea that the constant and prolonged cross-reference to BITs and case-law arising out of third-party BITs is a foundational element of a *de facto* multilateral system of investment law. In light of these considerations, it is arguable that arbitrators must thus act with a keen awareness of their role as both interpreters and creators of legal norms, ensuring that their decisions not only resolve the disputes before them but also contribute positively to the broader legal framework governing international investment. This dual role underscores the importance of a deep understanding of legal principles and a judicious approach to their application, as the interpretations made by arbitrators can have far-reaching implications beyond the immediate parties to a dispute.

Such a duty, however, is often contested as a form of judicial (*rectius*, arbitral) activism, criticised by some as an excess of the mandate conferred by the parties to the arbitrators.[16] However, I would argue that this phenomenon is almost inevitable in investment arbitration, as it stems from two primary factors. First, the professional backgrounds of many arbitrators play a crucial role. Arbitrators often come from distinguished careers as legal scholars, judges or practitioners in international law, bringing with them a deep understanding of legal principles and a commitment to advancing the coherence and development of the law.[17] Their extensive experience and

15 *Ibid.*

16 Bjorklund, 'Are arbitrators (judicial) activists?', *supra*, Chapter 1, note 1; Alcolea, 'Arbitral Activism and Choice of Law under the ICSID Convention', *supra*, Chapter 1, note 23; Lam, 'Legal interpretation and adjudicatory activism in international commercial arbitration', 236–255; Hofmann, Schill, and Tams, *Preferential Trade and Investment Agreements – From Recalibration to Reintegration*, 9.

17 Most arbitrators tend to share a few other characteristics based on gender, ethnicity, age and ability, which I will not address here for reasons of pertinence. The matter has been extensively investigated in the scholarship, thus I will refer the reader to Puig, 'Social capital in the arbitration market', *supra*, Chapter 3, note 2. See also D'Silva,

expertise naturally influence their interpretive approach, leading them to engage in more active law-making to address the complexities and gaps they encounter in the treaties and cases before them. This academic and scholarly background influenced, in particular, arbitrators' approaches to interpreting BIT clauses, leading to a more detailed and expansive clarification of treaty provisions.[18] For instance, the development of the *Salini* criteria, which articulate the requirements for an investment under the ICSID Convention, exemplifies the detailed interpretative work undertaken by such arbitrators.[19] Similarly, the precise definitions of key standards such as Most Favoured Nation treatment,[20] National Treatment,[21]

'Dealing in power: gatekeepers in arbitrator appointment in international commercial arbitration', 605–634; Nottage, Teramura, and Tanna, 'Developing diversity within diversity discourse: remembering non-lawyers in arbitration', 101–118; Franck, Freda, Lavin, Kellen, and Aaken, 'The Diversity Challenge: Exploring the Invisible College of International Arbitration', 429–506; Bjorklund, Behn, Franck, Giorgetti, Kidane, Nanteuil, and Onyema, 'The Diversity Deficit in International Investment Arbitration', 410–440; Giorgetti, 'Who decides who decides in international investment arbitration', *supra*, Chapter 2, note 16; Polonskaya, 'Diversity in the investor-state arbitration: Intersectionality must be a part of the conversation', 259–298; Greenwood and Mark Baker, 'Is the balance getting better? An update on the issue of gender diversity in international arbitration', 413–442.

18 Langford, Behn, and Lie, 'The revolving door in international investment arbitration', 301–332; Ridi and Schultz, *Empirically Mapping Investment Arbitration Scholarship: Networks, Authorities, and the Research Front*; Charlotin, 'The place of investment awards and WTO decisions in international law: a citation analysis', 279–299; Schneiderman, 'Legitimacy and Reflexivity in International Investment Arbitration: A New Self-Restraint?', 471–495; Alschner, 'Ensuring Correctness or Promoting Consistency? Tracking Policy Priorities in Investment Arbitration through Large-Scale Citation Analysis'; Schultz, and Ridi, 'Arbitration literature', 1–32; Vargiu, 'Stakeholders of Investment Arbitration: establishing a dialogue among arbitrators, states, investors, academics and other actors in international investment law', *supra*, Chapter 1, note 1, p. 6; Böckstiegel, 'Commercial and investment arbitration: how different are they today?: The Lalive lecture', 577–590; Schreuer, Malintoppi, Reinisch, and Sinclair, *The ICSID Convention: A Commentary*, *supra*, Chapter 1, note 21, 626.

19 Salini v. Morocco, *supra*, Chapter 1, note 20.

20 *Supra*, Chapter 2, note 63.

21 An excellent overview of the development of the substantive content of the NT is provided by Leila Choukroune, 'National Treatment in International Investment Law and Arbitration: A Relative Standard for Autonomous Public Regulation and Sovereign Development', in Sanders, *The Principle of National Treatment in International Economic Law: Trade, Investment and Intellectual Property*, 183–219. See also Sornarajah, *The International Law on Foreign Investment*, *supra*, Chapter 1, note 12, 416–462; Reinisch, 'National Treatment', 846–869; Bjorklund, 'National Treatment', *supra*, Chapter 1, note 13, 29–58.

Fair and Equitable Treatment,[22] and the international minimum standard have been significantly shaped by arbitrators' interpretative efforts. These detailed interpretations have provided much-needed clarity and consistency in the application of vague treaty provisions, contributing to the development of a more coherent body of international investment law. The shift towards commercial law practitioners as arbitrators, some of whom have opted to become full-time arbitrators to avoid conflicts of interest, marks a notable change in the professional landscape.[23] However, the legacy of the contributions made by academically inclined arbitrators remains evident in the foundational concepts and standards that continue to guide investment arbitration. This historical context underscores how the interpretative duties of arbitrators, influenced by their academic and professional backgrounds, have been instrumental in shaping the legal framework governing international investments. Far from being solely a manifestation of arbitral activism, I would argue that this prolific interpretative activity reflects a necessary and constructive response to the ambiguities and generalities inherent in early BITs, ensuring that these treaties operate effectively in arbitral proceedings.

Second, the inherent vagueness and generality of most BITs signed before the mid-2000s necessitate a more expansive interpretative role. Many of these earlier BITs were drafted with broad, ambiguous language, reflecting a desire to attract foreign investment without committing to precise legal obligations. This vagueness left significant room for interpretation, requiring arbitrators to clarify and define the scope and application of treaty provisions in the context of specific disputes.[24] The shift from 2004 onwards, with states increasingly issuing new Model BITs, aimed to address these ambiguities by

---

22 *Supra*, Chapter 2, note 75.

23 Without casting any judgment on the implications, it is undeniable that the influence of commercial lawyers, who have seen a dramatic increase in appointments as arbitrators in investment disputes, has recently began to shape, or re-shape, the interpretation of certain provisions in BITs, which are in fact intended as instruments of public international law. See generally Houtte and Brunetti, 'Investment arbitration – ten areas of caution for commercial arbitrators', *supra*, Chapter 2, note 14; Sasson, 'Investment Arbitration: Procedure', *supra*, Chapter 3, note 21, 1288–1372; García-Bolívar, 'Comparing Arbitrator Standards of Conduct in International Commercial, Trade and Investment Disputes', 76–79; Sornarajah, 'The Retreat of Neo-Liberalism in Investment Treaty Arbitration', 273–296.

24 See generally Catharine Titi, 'The arbitrator as a lawmaker: Jurisgenerative processes in investment arbitration', *supra*, Chapter 3, note 8, pp. 833–836.

providing clearer and more detailed provisions.[25] Nonetheless, the legacy of earlier treaties continues to demand that arbitrators engage in substantial interpretative work to render coherent and just decisions. Thus, what might be perceived as judicial activism or overreach is, in reality, a necessary response to the indeterminate nature of earlier investment treaties and the sophisticated legal backgrounds of those who arbitrate these disputes. Far from being an exercise in self-aggrandisement, the interpretive duty of arbitrators is therefore a critical aspect of their role in ensuring that the international investment law regime functions effectively and fairly.

This second point is intrinsically connected to the first: the perceived 'arbitral activism' arises from the absence of precise definitions in investment treaties which mirrors a certain degree of flexibility or indeterminate language not unfamiliar in the tradition of international treaties. However, early and 1990s BITs, as stated beforehand, are particularly notable for their considerable degree of flexibility. This lack of specificity necessitates a more active interpretative role by arbitrators. In these earlier treaties, provisions were often drafted in broad, general terms to accommodate a wide range of investment scenarios and to attract foreign investors without imposing stringent legal obligations on host states.[26] Consequently, arbitrators are frequently called upon to clarify and define the scope and application of these vague treaty provisions to resolve specific disputes effectively. This need for interpretation has led to arbitrators playing a *quasi*-legislative role, where their decisions not only resolve the immediate disputes but also contribute to the broader understanding and development of international investment law. The lack of detailed definitions in these treaties means that arbitrators must engage deeply with the text and context of the provisions, drawing upon principles of international law, previous arbitral decisions and relevant legal scholarship to fill the gaps left by the treaty drafters. One may in fact argue that the flexibility inherent in early BITs places a significant interpretative burden on arbitrators, requiring them to balance the need for

25 The 2004 US Model BIT was immediately adopted as a template for the now replaced Netherlands Model BIT 2004, the Canada Model BIT 2004, the France Model BIT 2006, Germany Model BIT 2008, Austria Model BIT 2008, the United Kingdom Model BIT 2008 and the now replaced Colombia Model BIT 2008. These model instruments and those drafted after 2008 are available on the UNCTAD website at https://investmentpolicy.unctad.org/international-investment-agreements/model-agreements.

26 Salacuse, *The Law of Investment Treaties*, *supra*, Chapter 1, note 11, 96–168; Hepburn, Paparinskis, Poulsen, and Waibel, 'Investment law before arbitration', 929–947.

legal certainty with the flexible nature of treaty language. This balance is crucial in maintaining the legitimacy and effectiveness of the international investment regime.

3.2. The *De Facto* Doctrine of Precedent in International Investment Law

In theory, each arbitral award is binding only on the parties involved in that particular dispute.[27] However, as stated beforehand,[28] arbitral awards have long been used as persuasive precedent, particularly in the context of investment arbitration. This practice is less common in international commercial arbitration due to the high level of confidentiality typically associated with such cases: these awards often only become known to the public at the enforcement stage, when they are scrutinised by the courts of the seat of enforcement. The confidential nature of commercial arbitration means that awards do not frequently circulate beyond the parties involved, strictly limiting their role as precedential guidance in future disputes; in fact, most of the persuasive precedent in commercial arbitration comes from the judgement of high courts in cases of challenges to the enforcement of the award. By contrast, investment arbitration operates under a different paradigm, where the use of previous awards as persuasive precedent is a well-established practice. This difference arises because investment arbitration awards are routinely published, and recent calls for increased transparency have led to the publication of not only the awards themselves

27 Article 54 of the ICSID Convention states that '[e]ach Contracting State shall recognize an award rendered pursuant to this Convention as binding and enforce the pecuniary obligations imposed by that award within its territories as if it were a final judgment of a court in that State', a somehow more convoluted provision than others like Article 32 of the UNCITRAL Arbitration Rules, which simply defines the arbitral award as 'final and binding on the parties', or Article 40 of the SCC Arbitration Rules provide for any award to be 'final and binding on the parties when rendered'. In any event, the finality of arbitral awards, and the fact that awards only express their effects on the parties to the dispute in which they were rendered, is widely accepted and not seriously debated. See *ex multis* Park and Paulsson, 'The Binding Force of International Arbitral Awards', 253–286; Clapham, 'Finality of investor-state arbitral awards: has the tide turned and is there a need for reform?', 437–466; Platt, 'The appeal of appeal mechanisms in international arbitration: fairness over finality?', 531–560; Mandelbaum, 'The Measure of Finality: A Dialectal Analysis of Legitimacy Concerns in International Investment Arbitration', 1–25.

28 See *supra*, Chapter 1, Chapter 3.1. and Chapter 1, note 19 for a brief overview on the scholarship on the topic of the *de facto* system of precedent in investment arbitration.

but also numerous procedural decisions made during the course of arbitral proceedings.[29] As a result, there is a wealth of publicly accessible material that parties and arbitrators can reference. The relative transparency in investment arbitration thus fosters a system in which referring to previous awards has become customary. Arbitrators and legal scholars routinely cite past awards in their proceedings and analyses, and this practice is so ingrained that it is seldom questioned; there is an implicit acceptance that a body of precedents exists and should be considered in future arbitrations.[30] This system of precedent is not formally codified in the same way as judicial precedent in common law systems, but its practical effect is similar.[31] Arbitrators look to previous decisions for guidance on interpreting treaty provisions, applying legal principles and resolving specific factual scenarios. This reliance on past awards helps to promote consistency and predictability in investment arbitration, as it allows parties to anticipate how similar issues might be resolved based on established interpretations. Moreover, the constant practice of the publication of awards and procedural decisions has undoubtedly enhanced the often-questioned legitimacy of the investment arbitration system by providing a certain degree of transparency and accountability. Stakeholders, including states, investors and the broader public, can scrutinise the reasoning and outcomes of arbitrations, fostering trust in the fairness and integrity of the process. The widespread acceptance of using previous awards as persuasive precedent also reflects a certain need

29 Within the ICSID framework, the term 'decision' typically refers to rulings made by the tribunal on procedural or substantive issues during the course of the arbitration proceedings. These can include decisions on jurisdiction, admissibility of evidence, interim measures, or other procedural matters. Decisions are usually issued as part of the tribunal's efforts to manage the arbitration process and ensure that the proceedings move forward in an orderly manner. The term 'award' only refers to the final ruling by the tribunal that resolves the substantive issues of the dispute between the parties. The award addresses the merits of the case and determines the rights and obligations of the parties. Only the award is binding on the parties and is intended to bring the arbitration to a conclusion. However, one of the most important persuasive precedents in investment arbitration comes, in fact, from a decision: the reference is to the afore-mentioned *Salini* criteria, which come from the Tribunal's Decision on Jurisdiction of 31 July 2001 (see *supra*, Chapter 1, note 20).

30 Schill, *The Multilateralization of International Investment Law*, *supra*, Chapter 3, note 5, p. 365.

31 On the influence on the common law *stare decisis* doctrine on international law see Florczak-Wątor, *Constitutional Law and Precedent: International Perspectives on Case-based Reasoning.*

for coherence in international investment law. Given the complex and often contentious nature of investment disputes, a consistent approach to legal interpretation and application helps to mitigate the risk of contradictory or unpredictable outcomes. This consistency is particularly important in a field where significant financial and sovereign interests are at stake, and where the legal principles involved can have far-reaching implications. The practice of referring to previous awards has also contributed dramatically to the development of international investment law.

I do not intend to question the legitimacy of this *de facto* system of precedent. It is established and serves its intended purposes, making its existence an undeniable fact within the context of investment arbitration.[32] My aim here is to examine the role of arbitrators and consider whether the presence of this *de facto* system of precedent imposes any additional implied duties on them. Arguably, it does not. Investment arbitrators are appointed by the disputing parties to resolve a specific conflict, and their primary duty of diligence is owed to these parties. While their decisions are likely to contribute to the broader body of international investment law and may be referenced in future disputes, this potential influence should not be their primary concern. Arbitrators have no obligation towards any third parties or even towards the disputing parties outside the specific context of the arbitration. The fact that their award might be used as precedent is a by-product of the arbitration

32 I did so in Vargiu, '*Langue* and *Parole* of Investment Law', *supra*, Chapter 1, note 19, p. 311: 'this position is not entirely convincing as it requires to assume that there are, in fact, multilateral structures and concerted treaty-making policies underlying international investment law, that justify 'the use of multilateral approaches to treaty interpretation by arbitral tribunals, including through the widespread use of arbitral precedent even across treaties'. I would rather argue that arbitral tribunals adopt *quasi*-multilateral approaches to treaty interpretation, and use arbitral precedent across treaties, to build these multilateral structures that not only do not actually exist (as proven by the lack of a substantive multilateral convention on investment regulation) but are also not necessarily desirable, as shown by the fact that the 'newer treaties' Schill refers to – reforming such multilateral structures – remain, in fact, negotiated and drafted on a bilateral or at best regional basis'. This passage extensively quotes Schill, 'MFN Clauses as Bilateral Commitments to Multilateralism: a Reply to Simon Batifort and J. Benton Heath', 914–935, and it is reported here for reasons of clarity and context: it is one thing to question the legitimacy of the dominant approach to interpretation and cross-referencing of BITs, and another to deny the practice. The aim of this book is to address the role of arbitrators within the existing system rather than theorizing a new one; therefore, the *de facto* system of precedent in investment arbitration is hereby treated as such: as a fact.

system, not an inherent feature or intended function of it. Consequently, there is no explicit or implicit obligation for arbitrators to consider how their decisions will fit into the broader system of precedent or to take future cases into account when drafting their awards. In fact, from a strictly formalistic perspective, arbitrators could disregard previous awards entirely when deciding the dispute before them. While such an approach might be considered controversial, and I would likely argue against it – given that Article 31 of the Vienna Convention on the Law of Treaties and Article 38 of the ICJ Statute suggest a degree of consideration for established norms and practices – this does not create an obligation for arbitrators to account for future disputes and tribunals in their deliberations.[33] Their mandate is confined to the specific case at hand, and their duty of diligence is directed towards delivering a fair and just resolution for the parties involved in that case alone. The broader implications of their awards, while significant, do not impose additional duties on the arbitrators themselves. Therefore, the presence of a *de facto* system of precedent in investment arbitration does not alter, *per se*, the fundamental duties of arbitrators. Their role remains focussed on resolving the disputes for which they have been appointed, applying the relevant laws and principles to the specific facts before them. The influence of their decisions on future cases is an incidental consequence of their work, not a guiding principle that should shape their decision-making process. A reliable system of *de facto* precedent fundamentally relies on sound reasoning, and investment arbitrators are expressly required to state the reasons upon which their awards are based, as stipulated by Article 52 of the ICSID Convention. This provision underscores that the failure to articulate the reasoning behind an award constitutes grounds for annulment. While this obligation ensures that awards are well-founded and transparent, however, it does not extend to requiring arbitrators to consider how their reasoning might be evaluated by future tribunals. The arbitrators' duty to provide thorough and coherent reasoning is directed solely towards the parties involved in the dispute at

---

33 United Nations, Statute of the International Court of Justice, 18 April 1946. Article 38(1) of the Statute famously states that '[t]he Court, whose function is to decide in accordance with international law such disputes as are submitted to it, shall apply [...] judicial decisions [...] as subsidiary means for the determination of rules of law'. See for further considerations Borda, 'The use of precedent as subsidiary means and sources of international criminal law', 65–82; Petersmann, 'The judicial task of administering justice in trade and investment law and adjudication', 5–28; Tumonis, 'Judicial Creativity and Constraint of Legal Rules: Dueling Cannons of International Law', 93–133).

hand. Their focus must remain on resolving the specific issues before them with clarity and rigour, without being burdened by the potential future use of their awards as precedent.

3.3. Stating the Reasons upon Which the Award Is Based

Elaborating on this point, it is interesting to note that, while no obligation exists upon arbitrators to consider the role of their award in shaping the contours of international investment law, the express duty to state the reasons behind such awards has long-ranging consequences beyond merely explaining to the parties why the case has been decided in a particular manner. The reasoning detailed in the text of an award serves multiple significant purposes, some of which have been addressed earlier.[34] It is not solely the fulfilment of the duty to clarify the decision-making process of the tribunal for the parties, nor is it simply a requirement to prevent the annulment or setting aside of the award: stating the reasons behind the award also represents a rather significant manifestation of the aforementioned law-making activity of arbitrators, and is the driving force behind the evolution of investment law and the education of future investment lawyers. Articulating the tribunal's reasoning in an award also ensures that the decision is grounded in an existing legal framework, providing a certain degree of transparency and, I would argue, accountability in the proceedings. A detailed reasoning in the award not only clarifies the tribunal's interpretation of the BIT and the application of its provisions to the specific facts of the case but also contributes to the collective understanding and development of international investment law. Moreover, as stated beforehand, the duty to state reasons is expressly enshrined in Article 52 of the ICSID Convention, which lists the failure to state reasons as a ground for annulment. This requirement ensures that awards are not arbitrary and that parties can understand the legal basis of the merits of the award. However, there is a further issue, or implication, of this duty, that extends its scope far beyond the mere compliance with procedural requirements. If one considers investment law as a effectively multilateral system, the reasoning provided by arbitrators becomes part of a body of case-law that informs future arbitral decisions and legal scholarship. It is this practice of articulating detailed reasoning in awards that contributes to the aforementioned *de facto* system of precedent in investment arbitration. While arbitrators, as frequently reiterated in these pages, are not formally bound by previous decisions, they regularly refer to and

34 *Supra*, Chapter 2.3.

rely on the reasoning of prior awards to ensure consistency and predictability in their own decisions. This reliance on past awards has the potential to build a coherent and stable body of case-law, which is essential for maintaining the legitimacy and efficacy of the system of investment arbitration. As such, the reasoning in arbitral awards serves not only to resolve the specific dispute but also to contribute to the ongoing dialogue and development of legal standards and principles within the field. Furthermore, the detailed reasoning in awards is instrumental in educating and guiding future investment lawyers: it may be a trite thing to add, but practitioners, scholars and students closely study these awards to understand the application of international investment law in practice. A comprehensive analysis provided by arbitrators offers valuable insights into the interpretation of treaty provisions, the application of legal principles and the resolution of complex factual scenarios. While I would certainly not argue that there is a duty upon the arbitrators to also consider the educational function of arbitral awards, the fact that they will influence the current and the next generation of lawyers is likely a criterion against which an award could and should be tested by other arbitrators and scholars alike.

The reasoning behind an award, therefore, is not merely a procedural requirement or a safeguard against annulment: it is a fundamental aspect of the arbitrators' role in the broader context of international investment law. Because of this, the opinions of those who believe that arbitrators have a duty towards the entire international community may have some merit. Even if arbitrators only respond to the parties involved in their specific dispute, they are (or they should be) aware that their award will become part of a *de facto* multilateral system. This system, although composed of thousands of treaties, functions collectively to regulate international foreign investment and is recognised as such by all its stakeholders. Consequently, it would be myopic for arbitrators to disregard this broader context when interpreting applicable laws. The profound similarity between provisions in different BITs is reinforced by the fact that such provisions are generally drafted with similar outcomes in mind – namely, the regulation of specific aspects of the relationship between foreign investors and host states. Recognising this interconnectedness does not imply that arbitrators have an implicit duty to consider the entire system when drafting individual awards. However, part of their duty of diligence is to be knowledgeable about the existing body of case-law and to take it into account when making decisions. While it might be excessive to require arbitrators to consider the broader significance of their awards for the global investment law community, it is reasonable to expect them to be mindful that their decisions will be read and utilised by others beyond the immediate parties to the dispute. Arbitrators, therefore, operate within a dual framework. On one hand, they are tasked with resolving the specific dispute before them, adhering to the principles of impartiality and fairness.

On the other hand, they must acknowledge the broader implications of their awards within the international investment regime. This duality necessitates a careful akin to walking on a tightrope arbitrators must remain focussed on the parties' immediate concerns while being aware of the potential precedential value of their decisions. The duty of diligence mandated by the ICSID Convention and various arbitration rules entails a thorough understanding of previous awards and the jurisprudence they create. Arbitrators are expected to engage with prior decisions not only to ensure consistency but also to enhance the legitimacy and predictability of the arbitration process. This engagement is crucial because the principles and standards developed in past awards form a robust body of guidance for future cases. Moreover, this consideration of previous awards aligns with principles of legal certainty, assuring parties that similar cases will be treated similarly, and fostering a stable and predictable legal environment. For foreign investors and host states, this predictability is vital for making informed decisions and managing risks associated with cross-border investments. Nonetheless, the expectation that arbitrators should be aware of the broader impact of their awards does not equate to a direct obligation to shape their decisions with future cases in mind. Their primary duty remains to the parties before them. However, the awareness that their decisions will be scrutinised and possibly relied upon by future tribunals simply acts as a secondary layer of responsibility, to encourage arbitrators to articulate their reasoning clearly and comprehensively, ensuring that their decisions can withstand the test of time and scrutiny. This dual responsibility also underscores the importance of transparency in investment arbitration. The trend towards greater transparency, exemplified by the ever-increasing publication of awards and procedural decisions and the recent UNCITRAL Rules on Transparency in Treaty-Based Investor-State Arbitration,[35] serves multiple purposes, that could be summed up as enhancing the legitimacy of the arbitration process by allowing stakeholders to see and understand the *rationale* behind decisions.[36]

35 *Supra*, Chapter 2, note 11.

36 Indeed, Regulation 22 of the ICSID Administrative and Financial Regulations states that '[t]he Secretary-General shall appropriately publish information about the operation of the Centre, including the registration of all requests for conciliation or arbitration and in due course an indication of the date and method of the termination of each proceeding' and that '[i]f both parties to a proceeding consent to the publication of [...] arbitral awards or [...] the minutes and other records of proceedings, the Secretary-General shall arrange for the publication thereof, in an appropriate form with a view to furthering the development of international law in relation to investments'.

The interpretative role of arbitrator does not necessarily (or at least not always) imply arbitral activism, but rather a necessary and legitimate function within arbitral proceedings. This process of interpretation is essential for the evolution of international investment law, ensuring that it remains responsive to the changing dynamics of global economic relations. The notion that arbitrators should be conscious of the broader implications of their awards is thus reinforced by the interconnectedness of the international investment regime. The global nature of investment flows means that decisions in one jurisdiction can have ripple effects elsewhere. Arbitrators, therefore, must be attuned to the potential wider impact of their decisions, not in a prescriptive sense but as a matter of responsible adjudication. This awareness helps to ensure that their decisions contribute positively to the overall stability and fairness of the investment regime.

In conclusion, while arbitrators are not explicitly required to consider the broader implications of their awards for the international investment community, the duty of diligence implicitly encompasses an awareness of the existing body of case law and its potential influence. Arbitrators must strike a balance between their primary duty to resolve the specific dispute before them and the secondary responsibility to contribute to the continuity and coherence of international investment law. This dual role, facilitated by transparency and thorough reasoning, ensures that the arbitration process remains fair, predictable and legitimate. The interconnectedness of the international investment regime necessitates that arbitrators remain mindful of the broader context in which they operate; however, to argue that these aspects of the activity of an international investment arbitrator constitute objective duties or responsibility of arbitrators may be a step too far.

Chapter 4

BRIDGING THE GAP: ARBITRATORS AND THEIR RESPONSIBILITIES

4.1. The Backlash against Investment Arbitration

The backlash against investment law and arbitration has indeed been widespread and diverse in recent years, reflecting a variety of concerns and critiques from various quarters.[1] In particular, the mainstream debate on the Transatlantic Trade and Investment Partnership (TTIP) negotiations in 2013 brought investment arbitration into the limelight, igniting a critical campaign that was often both misguided and misdirected.[2] One of the most contentious aspects of this debate centred around the portrayal of investment arbitration tribunals as 'secret courts', a term that has become a rallying cry for critics despite its questionable accuracy.[3] This characterisation, while resonant with public sentiment, has fuelled a rather aggressive argument that investment

1 The expression is indeed taken from Waibel, Kaushal, Chung, and Balchin, *The Backlash against Investment Arbitration: Perceptions and Reality*, *supra*, Chapter 1, note 2; although the book was published prior to the events that brought investment arbitration under mass media scrutiny, the expression aptly captures the extensive criticism that has impacted investment arbitration over the past decade.

2 Transatlantic Trade and Investment Partnership (TTIP) – Documents, available at https://policy.trade.ec.europa.eu/eu-trade-relationships-country-and-region/countries-and-regions/united-states/eu-negotiating-texts-ttip_en.

3 See *ex multis* Hazel Sheffield, 'TTIP: UK Government found secret courts in trade deal have 'lots of risk and no benefit' in its only assessment'. *The Independent*, 27 April 2016, available at https://www.independent.co.uk/news/business/news/ttip-uk-government-only-did-one-assessment-of-trade-deal-and-found-it-had-lots-of-risks-and-no-benefit-a6999646.html; Nick Dearden, 'Corporate courts vs the environment', *Al Jazeera*, 2 August 2021, available at https://www.aljazeera.com/opinions/2021/8/2/corporate-courts-vs-the-environment; Arthur Nielsen, 'Revealed: secret courts that allow energy firms to sue for billions accused of 'bias' as governments exit, *The Guardian*, 14 November 2022, available at https://www.theguardian.com/business/2022/nov/14/revealed-secret-courts-that-allow-energy-firms-to-sue-for-billions-accused-of-bias-as-governments-exit; Lottie Limb, 'Inside the 'secretive' tribunals where fossil fuel

arbitration mechanisms inherently foster inequality and enable corporations to exploit developing countries, especially those in the Global South. Indeed, contrary to the traditionally dominant narrative that investment arbitration provides a neutral forum that can safeguard investors against expropriation and unfair treatment, thus fostering a stable investment climate that can contribute to economic development, its detractors contend that the system is fundamentally flawed, disproportionately favouring wealthy multinational corporations over the sovereign rights of states, particularly those with weaker bargaining power.[4]

The TTIP negotiations highlighted these tensions dramatically. Critics argued that the inclusion of investor-state dispute settlement mechanisms within TTIP would grant corporations excessive power to challenge public interest regulations, effectively undermining national sovereignty and democratic governance.[5] The term 'secret courts' gained traction as it encapsulated fears about the opacity and perceived lack of accountability within the arbitration process. While commercial arbitral proceedings are typically confidential to protect the interests of the parties involved, the same cannot be said – or at least not to the same extent – for investment arbitration; however, this perceived secrecy has been interpreted as a lack of transparency, fuelling suspicion and mistrust among the public and civil society organisations. Moreover, strong criticism argued that investment arbitration places an undue burden on

---

companies 'steal' from developing countries', *Euronews*, 19 November 2022, available at https://www.euronews.com/green/2022/11/19/inside-the-secretive-tribunals-where-fossil-fuel-companies-steal-from-developing-countries. For context, the case-law of the International Centre for Investment Disputes (ICSID), including pending cases, is publicly available at https://icsid.worldbank.org/cases/case-database.

4 Morosini and Badin, *Reconceptualizing International Investment Law from the Global South*; Ratner, 'International investment law through the lens of global justice', 747–775; Cutler and Lark, 'The hidden costs of law in the governance of global supply chains: the turn to arbitration', 29(3) 719–748; Perrone and Schneiderman, 'International economic law's wreckage: depoliticization, inequality, precarity', *Research Handbook on Critical Legal Theory* 446–472; Avayiwoe, 'Ensuring North-South Diversity in and Legitimacy of International Investment Arbitration: Africa in Perspective'. Questions about the effects of the system of investment law and arbitration on development and the economies in the Global South had already been formulated by Sornarajah, 'Power and justice in foreign investment arbitration', 103–140.

5 See generally Ville and Siles-Brügge, *T.T.I.P. : The Truth about the Transatlantic Trade and Investment Partnership*; Morin *The Politics of Transatlantic Trade Negotiations: TTIP in a Globalized World*; Eliasson and Huet, *Civil Society, Rhetoric of Resistance, and Transatlantic Trade*; Oleart, *Framing TTIP in the European Public Spheres: Towards an Empowering Dissensus for EU Integration.*

developing countries, which often lack the financial and legal resources to defend themselves effectively in arbitral proceedings. This can lead to substantial financial liabilities for developing countries, diverting resources away from critical public services and development projects. Furthermore, the fear is that the threat of costly arbitration claims may have a chilling effect on the ability of these countries to regulate in the public interest, especially in areas such as environmental protection, public health and labour standards.[6] The argument that investment arbitration creates inequality is also rooted in the broader context of global economic disparities. Developing countries, particularly those in the Global South, are often perceived as being at a disadvantage in the global investment landscape. The asymmetry in economic power between multinational corporations and sovereign states can lead to situations where the latter are compelled to enter into investment agreements that may not fully protect their interests. This power imbalance is seen as being exacerbated by the system of investment arbitration system, which, critics argue, tends to favour investors from developed countries.[7] It is important to acknowledge, however, that the debate is not entirely one-sided. Supporters of investment arbitration maintain that it is a vital tool for attracting foreign investment, which can drive economic growth and development in host countries, and argue that by providing a reliable mechanism for dispute resolution, investment arbitration helps to mitigate the risks associated with investing in politically and economically unstable regions. This, in turn, can lead to increased capital flows, job creation and technological transfer, which are essential for the development of many countries in the Global South.[8] Nevertheless, the critique that the system is biased towards investors is supported by empirical evidence suggesting that investors tend to win a significant proportion of cases. Additionally, the high costs associated with arbitration proceedings can be prohibitive for many states, further skewing the playing field in favour of wealthier investors. The perception of bias is compounded by the fact that many arbitrators come from similar elite legal backgrounds, which can create

6 *Supra*, Chapter 2, note 79.

7 See generally Schultz and Dupont, 'Investment arbitration: Promoting the rule of law or over-empowering investors?:A quantitative empirical study', *supra*, Chapter 2, note 65; Franck, 'Development and Outcomes of Investment Treaty Arbitration', 435–490; Harten, 'Arbitrator Behaviour in Asymmetrical Adjudication: An Empirical Study of Investment Treaty Arbitration, 211–268.

8 Blythe, 'The Advantages of Investor-State Arbitration as a Dispute Resolution Mechanism in Bilateral Investment Treaties', 273–290; Ovidiu, 'Advantages and Disadvantages of Transparency and Public Participation in Investment Arbitration', 16–27; Markert, 'Improving Efficiency in Investment Arbitration', 215–246.

concerns about impartiality and fairness.[9] The backlash against investment arbitration, therefore, reflects deeper anxieties about the fairness and equity of the global economic system and raises fundamental questions about the balance between protecting investors and safeguarding the sovereign rights of states to regulate in the public interest.

Indeed, one may look at investment arbitration and find a number of issues with it. First and foremost, unlike most international courts and tribunals, hearings are generally not public, and decisions and awards are published quite late, which means that transparency is not absolute. This lack of transparency has been a significant point of criticism. Although the Mauritius Convention on Transparency in Treaty-based Investor-State Arbitration[10] has partially rectified this by setting new standards for openness in arbitral proceedings, and the UNCITRAL Rules on Transparency aim at making the issue mainstream in investment arbitration,[11] the overall perception remains that the process is shrouded in secrecy.

Another critical issue, as stated beforehand, is the composition of arbitration tribunals. These tribunals are typically made up of lawyers appointed by the disputing parties, which raises questions about the impartiality and legitimacy of the panels. Critics argue that this method of appointment can lead to a conflict of interest, as arbitrators might feel a sense of obligation towards the parties that selected them. This perception is particularly strong when the tribunal is perceived as being composed predominantly by investors or individuals who regularly represent investors in other arbitrations. This situation can create a bias, or at least the appearance of bias, in favour of investors. The widespread perception is that these tribunals consistently rule in favour of investors, awarding them substantial sums in compensation. Whether this perception is entirely accurate or not, it significantly undermines the credibility of the system.[12]

The quantum of investment arbitral awards has also been a contentious issue. Over the years, the amounts awarded in these cases have grown exponentially, reaching unprecedented levels. Notable examples include the

---

9 Langford, Behn, and Lie, 'The revolving door in international investment arbitration', *supra*, Chapter 3, note 18.

10 United Nations, United Nations Convention on Transparency in Treaty-based Investor-State Arbitration, General Assembly resolution 69/116, 10 December 2014.

11 *Supra*, Chapter 2, note 10.

12 See *ex multis* Smith, 'Impartiality of the party-appointed arbitrator', 320–342; Nariman, 'Standards of Behaviour of Arbitrators', *supra*, Chapter 2, note 21; Donaubauer, Neumayer, and Nunnenkamp, 'Winning or losing in investor-to-state dispute resolution: the role of arbitrator bias and experience', 892–916.

Yukos arbitration, in which the tribunal awarded over $50 billion in damages,[13] and the *ConocoPhillips* case, in which the award was over $8 billion.[14] These so-called 'mega-awards' have sparked considerable debate regarding the legitimacy of crippling compensation.[15] The scale of these awards can indeed have significant financial implications for the respondent states, particularly those with limited resources, exacerbating existing economic inequalities and creating further grounds for criticism. The legal reasoning behind some of these awards has also been heavily scrutinised. Critics argue that tribunals sometimes adopt expansive interpretations of investment treaties, which can lead to disproportionately high compensation for investors.[16] This expansive interpretation can be seen in the way tribunals assess the Fair and Equitable Treatment standard or the concept of expropriation, often broadening these definitions in ways that favour investors. Such interpretations can increase the liabilities of states beyond what might have been anticipated when they entered into the treaties, thereby raising concerns about the predictability and stability of the system of investment arbitration. Another significant concern is the cost of arbitration proceedings. The high legal fees and administrative costs associated with arbitration can be prohibitive, particularly for developing countries. These costs can deter states from defending themselves robustly in arbitration, leading to settlements that might not reflect the true merits of the case.[17]

The appointment process for arbitrators is another area of concern. The pool of arbitrators tends to be relatively small and exclusive, often comprising the same individuals who rotate between acting as arbitrators and representing parties in other cases. This 'revolving door' phenomenon can create an insular community that may be perceived as lacking diversity

13 Yukos Universal Limited (Isle of Man) v. The Russian Federation, UNCITRAL, PCA Case No. 2005-04/AA227, Award, 18 July 2014.

14 ConocoPhillips Petrozuata B.V., ConocoPhillips Hamaca B.V. and ConocoPhillips Gulf of Paria B.V. v. Bolivarian Republic of Venezuela, ICSID Case No. ARB/07/30, Award of the Tribunal, 8 March 2019.

15 Paparinskis, 'A Case Against Crippling Compensation in International Law of State Responsibility', 1246–1286; Paparinskis, 'Crippling compensation in the International Law Commission and investor-state arbitration', 289–312).

16 ConocoPhillips v. Venezuela, *supra*, Chapter 4, note 14, Dissenting Opinion of Prof. Georges Abi-Saab.

17 Bottini, Titi, Aznar, Chaisse, Jovanovic, and Sola, 'Excessive Costs and Recoverability of Costs Awards in Investment Arbitration', 251–299; Franck, 'Rationalizing Costs in Investment Treaty Arbitration', 769–852; Hodgson, 'Costs in Investment Treaty Arbitration: The Case for Reform', 748–759.

and inclusiveness. The limited representation of arbitrators from different geographic regions, genders and legal traditions can lead to a lack of diverse perspectives in arbitration decisions, further fuelling criticisms about the legitimacy and fairness of the process.[18]

To address these issues, various reforms have been proposed, with variable degrees of success. These include increasing transparency by mandating the publication of all arbitration decisions and making hearings open to the public, ensuring a more balanced composition of arbitration panels by diversifying the pool of arbitrators, and capping the amounts that can be awarded in certain types of disputes to prevent excessive compensation. Additionally, there have been calls for the establishment of an appellate mechanism to review arbitration decisions, which could enhance the consistency and predictability of rulings.[19] Another proposed reform is the creation of a multilateral investment court to replace the current *ad hoc* arbitration system, which could provide a more structured and permanent forum for resolving investment disputes.[20]

4.2. A Defence of Investment Arbitration

Investment arbitration is a mechanism with no particular inspiration, being a derivative of international commercial arbitration. However, several peculiarities distinguish it from its commercial counterpart, making it a unique field with specific characteristics and challenges. First, in the system of investment arbitration, one of the parties involved is invariably a state, rather than a private law entity. This involvement of a sovereign state introduces a distinct set of legal and political considerations, as states must balance their commitments to foreign investors with their obligations to their citizens and their sovereign right to regulate. Second, the consent to arbitrate in investment disputes is not derived from a specific arbitration

---

18 Langford, Behn, and Lie, 'The revolving door in international investment arbitration', *supra*, Chapter 2, note 18.

19 *Supra*, Chapter 2, note 59.

20 See generally Bungenberg and Reinisch, *From Bilateral Arbitral Tribunals and Investment Courts to a Multilateral Investment Court: Options Regarding the Institutionalization of Investor-State Dispute Settlement*; Bungenberg and Reinisch, *Draft Statute of the Multilateral Investment Court*; Scheu and Schöttmer, *Creation and Implementation of a Multilateral Investment Court*, Baltag and Ana Stanič, *The future of Investment Treaty Arbitration in the EU Intra-EU BITs, the Energy Charter Treaty, and the Multilateral Investment Court*; Kaufmann-Kohler and Potestà, *The Composition of a Multilateral Investment Court and of an Appeal Mechanism for Investment Awards*; Garcia and Guven, 'Designing a Multilateral Investment Court for Procedural Justice', 461–486.

agreement negotiated between the disputing parties. Instead, it is based on a blanket consent given by the state in the arbitration clause embedded within bilateral investment treaties (BITs) or multilateral investment agreements. This pre-emptive consent means that a state agrees in advance to arbitrate disputes with investors from the other contracting state, even before any particular dispute arises. This system of pre-consent is crucial in fostering an environment of trust and predictability for foreign investors, who can be assured of a neutral forum for resolving disputes. Third, the applicable law in investment arbitration is fundamentally public international law. The treaties that form the basis for arbitral proceedings are international legal instruments, and their interpretation and application must conform to the principles of public international law. The Vienna Convention on the Law of Treaties serves as the primary interpretive tool, guiding how treaty provisions should be understood and applied. The Vienna Convention's rules on treaty interpretation emphasise the ordinary meaning of treaty terms, the context and the treaty's object and purpose, ensuring a coherent and systematic approach to the interpretation of investment treaties.[21] Furthermore, the system of investment arbitration often involves the interplay of various legal frameworks, including customary international law, general principles of law and relevant municipal laws. This complex legal landscape requires arbitrators to possess a nuanced understanding of both international and domestic legal systems, as well as the ability to reconcile conflicts between different legal norms. The public international law dimension also introduces considerations of state responsibility and the protection of public interests, which are less prominent in purely commercial arbitration contexts.

The enforcement of arbitral awards in investment disputes is another distinctive feature. Awards rendered under the auspices of the ICSID benefit from automatic enforcement in member states, as stipulated by the ICSID Convention. This means that ICSID awards are treated as final and binding, and they must be enforced as if they were a final judgment of a court in each member state.[22] This automatic enforcement mechanism significantly enhances the effectiveness of the system of investment arbitration, providing – regardless of what one may think about the justice of the system and *in* the system – a robust guarantee of compliance. For non-ICSID awards, enforcement is subject to the requirements of the New York Convention on the Recognition

21 See *supra*, Chapter 3.1.

22 See *supra*, Chapter 2, note 59.

and Enforcement of Foreign Arbitral Awards.[23] Article V of the New York Convention outlines limited grounds on which recognition and enforcement of an award may be refused, such as lack of due process, issues of arbitrability or contravention of public policy. While these grounds provide some safeguards against the enforcement of problematic awards, they also introduce a degree of uncertainty, as the interpretation of these grounds can vary between jurisdictions. Nonetheless, the New York Convention remains a cornerstone of the global arbitral framework, facilitating the cross-border enforcement of awards and thereby also supporting the stability of the investment environment.

The distinctive nature of investment arbitration also manifests in its procedural aspects. As it has been seen above, arbitral proceedings in investment disputes often involve a somehow higher degree of formality and complexity compared to commercial arbitration. This is partly due to the involvement of states and the public interest implications of the disputes. The procedural rules governing these proceedings, such as those of ICSID, UNCITRAL or other institutional rules, provide for a relatively structured process, including detailed provisions on jurisdiction, the conduct of proceedings and the issuance of awards. Moreover, the involvement of states as parties to the disputes introduces unique procedural dynamics. States may be subject to constitutional and administrative constraints that can affect their participation in arbitral proceedings. Issues such as sovereign immunity, state privileges and the need to protect sensitive information can complicate the arbitral process.

Are these differences radical in terms of the proceedings? I would argue that it is not the case. Investment arbitration remains a type of arbitration characterised mainly by its subject matter rather than by the procedure. As a mechanism, it remains rather neutral. From a fundamentally procedural perspective, both the foreign investor and the host state have an equal opportunity to come out of the case victorious, and they have the same opportunity to present their case, given that the award will be set aside if due process is not observed. The neutrality of investment arbitration is grounded in the principles of fairness and equality that underpin arbitral proceedings. Both parties, irrespective of their nature – be them a sovereign state or a private investor – are afforded equal procedural rights. This includes the right to select arbitrators, the right to present evidence, the right to cross-examine witnesses, and the right to submit legal arguments. These procedural safeguards are designed to ensure that both parties can fully and fairly present their case. Furthermore, arbitral proceedings in investment disputes are governed by well-established rules and protocols that emphasise procedural neutrality.

---

23 Also see *supra*, Chapter 2, note 70.

Institutions such as the ICSID and the UNCITRAL provide comprehensive procedural frameworks that arbitral tribunals must follow. These frameworks include detailed provisions on the constitution of the tribunal, the conduct of hearings, the submission of evidence and the issuance of awards. Moreover, the procedural equality in investment arbitration is reflected in the equal access to remedies and procedural recourse available to both parties. Both the foreign investor and the host state can challenge the arbitral award if they believe that their procedural rights have been violated. For instance, as it has been seen, under the ICSID Convention, either party can request the annulment of an award on specific grounds, such as a serious departure from fundamental procedural rules or the tribunal exceeding its powers. Similarly, under the New York Convention, parties can seek to resist the enforcement of an award on limited grounds, including procedural deficiencies. It is also worth noting that the procedural neutrality of investment arbitration extends to the transparency and accountability of the proceedings. Although investment arbitration has historically been criticised for its lack of transparency, recent reforms have sought to address these concerns. Initiatives such as the aforementioned Mauritius Convention on Transparency and the UNCITRAL Rules on Transparency in Treaty-based Investor-State Arbitration aim to increase the openness of arbitral proceedings. These reforms allowed for the publication of key documents, open hearings to the public and allow for the submission of *amicus curiae* briefs by non-disputing parties.

From a procedural perspective, investment arbitration is fundamentally designed to provide a level playing field for both the foreign investor and the host state. Despite the perception that investment arbitration may favour investors due to the high-profile cases often reported in the media, the procedural design of the system aims at being impartial. Both investors and states have won and lost cases, and the outcomes often depend on the specific facts and legal arguments presented in each case. At least in theory – and there is no evidence of the contrary – the arbitral tribunals, guided by principles of international law and procedural fairness, strive to deliver decisions that are just and equitable, based on the merits of each dispute.

The question of whether the backlash against investment arbitration is justified, therefore, merits careful consideration. It is evident that the outcomes of investment disputes are often unfavourable to host states, that the phenomenon of mega-awards presents significant challenges, and that adjudicating public law measures in relatively private settings raises concerns about the impact of arbitral awards on the populations of the host state. Furthermore, there is a perceived lack of accountability among arbitrators: errors in substantive law are not subject to appeal, and while poorly performing arbitrators may face difficulties in being reappointed, this is not guaranteed due to the absence of a regulatory authority overseeing appointments. Despite these concerns, it is crucial to determine whether these issues constitute systemic or structural flaws inherent in investment arbitration. The argument here is that they do not; rather, these are deficiencies stemming from the provisions of the ICSID Convention and BITs, as will be elaborated upon in the next section of this chapter.

First, the unfavourable outcomes for host states in some investment disputes should be viewed in context. While certain high-profile cases result in substantial damages and compensation awards issued against states, these are exceptions rather than the rule. Each case in investment arbitration is adjudicated on its individual merits, facts and applicable legal principles. The perception of bias is often fuelled by these few notable cases but does not reflect a consistent trend. Most disputes are resolved without extreme outcomes, and many are decided in favour of the host state. This indicates that the system does not systematically disadvantage states but rather operates on a case-by-case basis, aiming for fairness and justice. The issue of crippling compensation, while significant, should be understood as a reflection of the damages incurred by investors due to state actions; a problem would emerge should these awards be the norm, but that is not the case – at least for the time being. The principles of compensation in international law necessitate making investors whole for their losses, which can result in large sums.[24] Although these awards can be burdensome for states, especially developing ones, they are not arbitrary but are calculated based on economic damages. The scrutiny of these awards has led to calls for reform and more consistent methodologies in damage calculation, showing the system's capacity for self-correction and improvement. Concerns about the relative privacy of arbitral proceedings, especially when public law measures are at stake, have been partially addressed by recent reforms aimed at increasing transparency. The aforementioned UNCITRAL Rules on Transparency and the Mauritius Convention on Transparency have made significant strides in opening up arbitral proceedings to public scrutiny. These reforms, as mentioned beforehand mandate the publication of key documents and public hearings and allow for the submission of *amicus curiae* briefs, and are all measures that enhance the transparency and accountability of investment arbitration,

---

24 Aaken, 'Primary and Secondary Remedies in International Investment Law and National State Liability – A Functional and Comparative View', 722; Shelton, *Remedies in International Human Rights Law* 38; Marboe, 'Compensation and Damages in International Law', 723–759; Marboe, *Calculation of Compensation and Damages in International Investment Law* pp. 153 ff.

addressing criticisms regarding its opacity. The accountability of arbitrators remains a contentious issue, particularly given the lack of an appellate mechanism to address substantive errors. However, the current system does incorporate checks and balances, including the ability to challenge arbitrators for bias and seek annulment of awards on limited grounds under the ICSID Convention. Although these measures do not equate to full appellate review, they do provide mechanisms to address procedural and jurisdictional concerns. Furthermore, the reappointment of arbitrators is – or should be – influenced by their reputation and past performance, which indirectly promotes accountability. The absence of a regulatory authority overseeing arbitrator appointments and conduct is often seen as a weakness. Nevertheless, the flexibility in arbitrator appointments allows parties to select individuals with the necessary expertise for their specific dispute. This autonomy is fundamental to the arbitral system, ensuring that arbitrators are well-suited to resolve complex investment disputes. Although this can lead to the reappointment of arbitrators with mixed records, there is an increasing demand for diversity and higher ethical standards in arbitrator appointments, which can mitigate these deficiencies.

These identified issues – unfavourable outcomes for states, mega-awards, limited transparency and arbitrator accountability – are examples of how the perceived issues of investment arbitration do not constitute systemic flaws but rather deficiencies that can be addressed through targeted reforms.

4.3. The Problem with the Applicable Law

The preamble of the ICSID Convention clearly states that one of the primary motivations for its establishment was the recognition that disputes between foreign investors and host states, in the absence of 'international methods of settlement', would otherwise be subjected to national legal processes. The underlying rationale of investment arbitration is to remove investment disputes from the jurisdiction of national courts, which may be perceived as inherently biased in favour of the host state – the same entity of which these national courts are an expression.[25] This externalisation of dispute resolution aims to ensure neutrality and fairness in the adjudication of investment disputes. Recent studies, such as those by Perrone, suggest that investment arbitration may be part of a broader strategy to maintain the exploitation

---

25 Kaufmann-Kohler and Potestà, 'Why Investment Arbitration and Not Domestic Courts? The Origins of the Modern Investment Dispute Resolution System, Criticism, and Future Outlook', 7–29.

of natural resources in developing countries by corporations from Western states.[26] This perspective posits that the system of investment arbitration, embedded within a network of BITs, functions to protect the interests of these corporations, thereby perpetuating economic imbalances. While this view is subject to debate, it nonetheless underscores the profoundly significant role that BITs play in the global architecture of international investment law.

The chief instruments governing the regulation of foreign investment and the resolution of investment disputes are indeed the BITs, not the arbitral proceedings themselves. BITs establish the legal framework within which foreign investments are made and disputes are settled. They typically include substantive protections for investors, such as guarantees against expropriation, assurances of fair and equitable treatment, and provisions for the free transfer of capital. Additionally, BITs contain dispute resolution clauses that provide the consent of the contracting states to arbitrate investment disputes with investors from the other state party, thereby enabling arbitral proceedings to take place. Arbitral proceedings, in this context, are the mechanisms through which the substantive rules and protections enshrined in BITs are implemented and enforced. They serve as the procedural stage where the obligations and rights articulated in BITs are adjudicated. Thus, while investment arbitration is a crucial component of the dispute resolution landscape, its role is derivative: the mechanism operates within the parameters set by BITs from a substantive perspective, and the ICISD Convention or the applicable arbitration rules from a procedural standpoint.

This structural relationship highlights several key points. First, the criticisms directed at the system of investment arbitration often stem from the provisions and language of BITs. For instance, broad definitions of investment and expansive interpretations of investor protections in BITs can lead to outcomes that are viewed as overly favourable to investors. The arbitral tribunals are tasked with interpreting and applying these treaty provisions, and their decisions are influenced by the specific wording and intent of the BITs. Consequently, any perceived biases or imbalances in the system of investment arbitration are, to a significant extent, a reflection of the underlying treaty frameworks. Second, the neutrality and fairness of arbitral proceedings are fundamentally linked to the content and clarity of the BITs. Clear and precise treaty language can reduce ambiguities and limit the scope for expansive interpretations that may disadvantage host states. Therefore, improving the fairness and balance of the investment arbitration system

---

26 Perrone, *Investment Treaties and the Legal Imagination: How Foreign Investors Play by Their Own Rules*, *supra*, Chapter 1, note 27, pp. 96–121 in particular.

involves not only procedural reforms but also substantive changes to the BITs themselves. This includes revising treaty provisions to ensure a more equitable balance between investor protections and the regulatory autonomy of host states. Third, the enforcement of arbitral awards, while a critical aspect of the system, is governed by international conventions such as the ICSID Convention and the New York Convention. These conventions facilitate the recognition and enforcement of arbitral awards across jurisdictions, thus providing investors with a reliable mechanism to seek redress, but the grounds for challenging and refusing enforcement of awards are limited – an aspect that can keep substantively questionable awards within the system.

Furthermore, the involvement of states in BIT negotiations and their consent to arbitrate disputes underscore the consensual nature of the system. Host states, by entering into BITs, agree to certain limitations on their sovereign rights in exchange for the potential benefits of foreign investment. This agreement is predicated on the expectation that foreign investors will be afforded protections that national legal systems may not guarantee. However, the balance of these agreements can be tilted by power asymmetries that ultimately influence the terms of the BITs and the resultant arbitral decisions. The term 'Bilateral Investment Treaty' often serves as a convenient shorthand, but it can obscure the full implications of these agreements, which are more accurately described by their actual name – any variation of 'Bilateral Agreements for the Promotion and Protection of Investments'. The terminology itself is revealing: BITs are fundamentally designed to protect investors and promote investment flows between the contracting states. They are not instruments of social justice, nor are they primarily aimed at balancing the interests of foreign investors with those of host states. Instead, their primary purpose is to provide robust guarantees to investors and delineate the grounds on which investors can seek compensation for state actions that negatively impact their investments. BITs typically include several key provisions that underscore their protective nature. These provisions often encompass guarantees of fair and equitable treatment, protection from expropriation without adequate compensation, the free transfer of funds and most-favoured-nation treatment. Such clauses are designed to create a stable and predictable investment environment by ensuring that investors' rights are safeguarded against arbitrary or discriminatory actions by the host state. The emphasis is unequivocally on securing the interests of investors, providing them with legal remedies should their investments be adversely affected by state measures. One significant aspect of BITs is their approach to expropriation. Expropriation clauses in BITs typically provide that any direct or indirect expropriation must be accompanied by prompt, adequate and effective compensation. This principle is intended to protect investors from state actions that could unjustly deprive them of their investments. The notion of indirect expropriation, in particular, has expanded over time to include regulatory actions that, while not directly taking ownership of the investment, significantly diminish its value. This broad interpretation can cover a wide range of state measures, potentially encompassing legitimate public policy actions aimed at health, safety or environmental protection.[27]

The interpretation of BIT provisions has indeed broadened over the years, leading to increasingly expansive readings of investor protections. Arbitral tribunals have played a central role in this process, often interpreting the standards of treatment in ways that extend the scope of protections afforded to investors. For instance, the Fair and Equitable Treatment standard has been interpreted to include a broad array of state actions that might be seen as unfair, such as changes in the regulatory environment or failure to provide a stable and predictable investment climate. Such interpretations can impose significant constraints on the regulatory autonomy of host states, limiting their ability to implement policies that may adversely impact investors, even if those policies serve important public interests. The compensation amounts awarded in arbitral proceedings have also increased over time, reflecting the broadening interpretation of BIT protections. These so-called 'mega-awards' often result from complex calculations that take into account not only the direct losses incurred by investors but also the potential future profits lost due to state actions.[28] While these awards are intended to fully compensate investors for their losses, they can impose substantial financial burdens on host states, particularly those with limited fiscal capacity; this can indeed exacerbate existing economic inequalities and create significant political and social challenges within the host state.

It is important to reiterate that the expansive interpretation of BITs and the resultant high compensation awards are not arbitrary but are rooted in the legal framework established by the BITs themselves. The broad language of many BITs allows for wide-ranging interpretations, which arbitrators

27 Escarcena, *Indirect Expropriation in International Law*; Vargiu, 'Environmental Expropriation in International Investment Law', 213–238; Maria Daza-Clark, *International Investment Law and Water Resources Management: An Appraisal of Indirect Expropriation*; Riffel, 'Indirect Expropriation and the Protection of Public Interests', *supra*, Chapter 2, note 77; Godinez, 'A Case Note on the ICSID Tribunal's Decision in Hydro and Others v. Albania: Indirect Expropriation and Proportionality', 225–250.

28 Hansen, '"Missing Links" in Investment Arbitration: Quantification of Damages to Foreign Shareholders', 434–479; Parish, Newlson, and Rosenberg, 'Awarding moral damages to respondent states in investment arbitration', 225–245; Beharry and Bräutigam, 'Damages and valuation in international investment arbitration', *supra*, Chapter 3, note 6, 1423–1454.

apply based on the principles of international investment law. The protective intent of these treaties is clear: they are designed to mitigate risks for investors by providing strong legal guarantees and effective remedies. This focus on investor protection reflects the economic rationale behind BITs, which is to attract foreign investment by reducing the uncertainties and risks associated with investing in foreign jurisdictions. This book is not the stage to speculate upon or recommend what reforms could address these concerns. BITs could explicitly exclude certain types of regulatory measures from the scope of expropriation clauses or clarify the meaning of fair and equitable treatment to prevent overly broad interpretations. Additionally, the inclusion of exceptions for public policy measures related to health, safety and the environment could help ensure that BITs do not unduly constrain state regulatory powers. These are all features of the new generation of BITs, the effects of which will be tested in future arbitral cases, but the efficacy of which does not depend on arbitration as a mechanism, nor, likely, on the arbitrators called to interpret these provisions. What, then, should arbitrators be expected to do?

4.4. What Could Be Asked of Arbitrators?

In the previous chapters of this book, both the express duties and responsibilities of arbitrators, as well as their implied duties, have been thoroughly examined. As it has been shown, alongside the responsibilities outlined in the ICSID Convention and the arbitration rules most commonly adopted in investment arbitration, arbitrators possess a more general duty to understand, interpret and apply the law in accordance with the demands of their professional position and expertise – essentially, in line with the reasons for their appointment. It is, however, challenging to establish an express duty for arbitrators to act with consideration of their role within the global investment law system. One could certainly argue that this consideration is an inherent part of their role, to some extent, and that when they issue an award, they should take into account not only existing persuasive precedent but also the potential for their award to contribute to such precedent. Nonetheless, this notion of a 'moral' responsibility does not equate to a 'legal' obligation. In the absence of a clear legal mandate requiring arbitrators to conduct themselves in a particular manner, it is untenable to argue that they have an obligation to act as though they were judges within a common law system. The lack of a formal legal duty for arbitrators to consider their broader role in the investment law system stems from the nature of arbitral proceedings and the specific mandates provided to arbitrators. Unlike judges in a common law system, who operate within a hierarchical judicial structure and are bound by the principle of *stare decisis*, arbitrators in investment arbitration function within a more flexible and *ad hoc* framework. Their primary duty is to resolve the dispute before them based on the applicable law and the specific terms of the arbitration agreement or treaty. While arbitrators may draw upon past decisions as persuasive authority, they are not legally bound to follow precedent in the same way that judges in common law jurisdictions are.

Many arbitrators are aware of their influential role within the international investment law framework, and they strive to render awards that contribute to the development of a coherent and consistent body of jurisprudence; but have they got to do so? The notion of a 'moral' responsibility for arbitrators to consider the broader impact of their decisions is not without merit. Arbitrators, particularly those who frequently serve in investment disputes, understand that their awards can shape the expectations and behaviours of both investors and states. By issuing well-reasoned decisions that reflect a deep understanding of the underlying principles of international investment law, arbitrators can enhance the legitimacy and stability of the system. However, translating this moral responsibility into a legal obligation would require significant changes to the current arbitral framework.

As things stand, the situation is quite different. The role of a judge is almost sacred, as a judge theoretically embodies the state's monopoly on the administration of justice. Judges are appointed or elected to uphold the law impartially, often serving as nameless representations of judicial authority and integrity. They are bound by strict ethical standards and institutional frameworks designed to ensure their impartiality and independence. The role of the arbitrator, conversely, is inherently more personal. Arbitrators are chosen by the disputing parties specifically because of their professional reputation, expertise and experience. Their appointment is not quite the result of public trust in a judicial institution, but rather the outcome of a private selection process essentially aimed at securing a qualified opinion on a legal dispute: arbitrators are, in essence, hired by the parties to provide a resolution to a dispute based on their specialised knowledge and interpretative skills. Their opinion only becomes 'law' because of Article 53(1) in the context of the ICSID, or once it is incorporated in an enforcement judgment for non-ICSID cases. This essentially professional engagement contrasts starkly with the role of judges, who are vested with the authority to administer justice within a public law system. Using the term 'justice' in the context of investment arbitration is, therefore, quite problematic: is the primary aim of the system of investment arbitration to administer justice in a broad societal sense? Or it is, more correctly, to simply settle disputes between foreign investors and host states? This distinction is crucial because it underscores the fundamentally different objectives of arbitral proceedings compared to judicial proceedings. The concept of justice in a public judicial system involves a comprehensive consideration of fairness, equity and the broader public interest. Judges are expected to interpret and apply the law in ways that uphold these principles, ensuring that their decisions reflect societal values and norms. In contrast, the system of investment arbitration is primarily concerned with the specific legal rights and obligations of the parties involved in a dispute. While fairness and due process are important, the broader concept of justice as understood in public law is not the primary focus. Instead, the goal is to provide a binding resolution based on the legal and factual issues presented by the parties. Arbitrators, therefore, function more as highly qualified legal experts rather than judges. They are tasked with applying the highest standards of legal knowledge and interpretation, drawing on their expertise to resolve complex international disputes. However, their role does not carry the same institutional weight or public responsibility as that of a judge. There is no formal legal basis to treat arbitrators as judges because they operate within a fundamentally different framework. The legitimacy of their decisions derives from the consent of the parties and the specific rules governing the arbitration, rather than from a public mandate to administer justice.

This distinction has practical implications for how arbitrators conduct themselves and how their decisions are perceived. Unlike judges, who must navigate the constraints and expectations of a public judicial system, arbitrators are often afforded more flexibility in their approach to dispute resolution. They can tailor their proceedings to the needs and preferences of the parties, often leading to more efficient and specialised outcomes. However, this flexibility also means that arbitrators are subject to different standards of accountability. While they must adhere to ethical guidelines and maintain their professional integrity, their decisions are not subject to the same level of public scrutiny or appellate review as judicial decisions. The personal nature of the arbitrator's role also affects the dynamics of arbitral proceedings.[29]

29 One should always bear in mind that the efficacy of arbitration as a genuine dispute resolution mechanism hinges on several critical factors. The decision-making processes of arbitrators play a central role, as does their ability to manage the arbitral process effectively. Moreover, bias, self-deception, and vested interests in judgment and decision-making are persistent concerns that can undermine fairness. Cultural differences further complicate the evaluation of arguments, while psychological influences can affect witness testimony. The composition of the tribunal itself impacts decision-making, with diverse panels potentially offering more balanced judgments. The professional context of arbitration influences both arbitrators and legal counsel, shaping their approaches and strategies. Finally, developing methods for arbitrators and legal counsel to manage the arbitral process more effectively is essential for ensuring just and efficient resolutions. These aspects are thoroughly addressed in Tony Cole (ed.), *The Roles of Psychology in International Arbitration*, Wolters Kluwer, 2017.

Parties choose arbitrators based on their perceived expertise and reliability, often seeking individuals who have a track record of competence and fairness in similar cases. This selection process is inherently subjective, relying on the reputations and professional networks of the arbitrators. As a result, the quality and consistency of arbitral awards can vary, depending on the arbitrators' individual interpretations and the specific circumstances of each case. This variability underscores the importance of selecting arbitrators with the highest standards of professionalism and expertise.

Given these differences, it is essential to recognise that the system of investment arbitration serves a distinct function within the broader context of international law. Should one then expect arbitrators to be the motors of change in investment law, or to consider broader societal issues when adjudicating disputes between investors and states? As controversial and disappointing as it may be, the answer is no, because it is not within their remit. One may legitimately argue that the investment law regime is fundamentally skewed, favouring the interests of foreign investors over the welfare of host states and their populations. Indeed, investment law has historically facilitated the exploitation of natural, physical and economic resources in developing countries since the early stages of decolonisation and continues to do so. However, the scope of arbitrators' powers is rather limited. Article 42(3) of the ICSID Convention allows arbitrators to decide *ex aequo et bono* but only if the parties explicitly agree to this approach. In the absence of such agreement, arbitrators must apply the applicable law, which generally consists of BITs, relevant international law and occasionally domestic law. These legal instruments are designed primarily to protect investors, not to shield states from exploitation or to balance the interests of investors and states. Thus, arbitrators are bound to interpret and apply these laws, adhering to the specific mandates provided within the treaties and agreements governing the dispute. The primary role of arbitrators is to resolve disputes based on the specific legal and factual issues at hand, not to address broader societal concerns. This distinction is essential, as arbitration is a private method of dispute resolution focussed on the terms agreed by the parties and the applicable legal framework. Expecting arbitrators to act as agents of systemic change disregards their fundamental role and the constraints within which they operate.

The unbalanced nature of investment law, which many critics argue facilitates exploitation, is rooted in the historical and economic contexts in which these treaties were developed. BITs and similar agreements emerged during a period when developing countries sought to attract foreign investment to stimulate economic growth and development. The protections offered to investors were seen as essential to mitigate the risks associated with investing in politically and economically unstable regions. However, these protections can constrain the ability of states to regulate in the public interest. Reforming the investment law regime to address these imbalances requires action at the level of treaty negotiation and drafting, not within individual arbitral proceedings. States, as the primary architects of BITs, must take the initiative to renegotiate and revise these treaties to incorporate provisions that better balance investor protection with the right of states to pursue legitimate public policy objectives. This could include clarifying the scope of key treaty provisions, such as the fair and equitable treatment standard, to ensure they do not unduly restrict regulatory space or incorporating explicit exceptions for measures taken to protect public health, the environment and other critical areas. The development of new multilateral frameworks for investment protection and dispute resolution could also help address systemic issues in the current regime. Proposals for a multilateral investment court aim to create a more structured and transparent system for resolving investment disputes, with mechanisms for appellate review and enhanced procedural safeguards. Such reforms could help ensure greater consistency and fairness in arbitral decisions, addressing some of the criticisms of the current system.

In conclusion, while arbitrators play a crucial role in the resolution of investment disputes, I do not believe that they are actually positioned to drive systemic change in investment law. Their mandate is limited to applying the applicable law as defined by the relevant treaties and agreements. Addressing the fundamental imbalances in the investment law regime requires concerted efforts by states to reform the underlying legal frameworks. This includes renegotiating BITs, developing new multilateral instruments and ensuring that investment treaties better reflect the need for a balanced approach that protects both investor interests and the sovereign right of states to regulate in the public interest. Arbitrators, by adhering to their professional duties and applying the highest standards of legal interpretation, can contribute to the fairness and legitimacy of arbitral proceedings, but they cannot unilaterally rectify the systemic issues that characterise the current regime. The responsibility for achieving a more equitable investment law system ultimately lies with the states that negotiate and implement these treaties.

Chapter 5
CONCLUDING REMARKS

When arbitrators take it upon themselves to adopt an unsanctioned approach that effectively transforms a regime based on bilateral treaties into a *de facto* multilateral one, as argued by Schill, their responsibilities arguably extend beyond the specific dispute they are hearing to encompass the entire regime and its stakeholders. Given the absence of treaty provisions establishing such duties, and considering the unconventional evolution of investment law since the first international instruments on investment protection, one has two options: one is to re-examine the issues arising in investment law and arbitration from a different perspective that takes into account the societal implications of investment arbitral awards; the other approach is to focus on the interpretation of the applicable law, without considering external factors.[1] The latter approach, which considers the law as a social phenomenon, is not necessarily incorrect; in fact, such an outlook recognises the inherent nature of law as a construct that does not function in isolation. Law, by its very essence, is interwoven with the fabric of society and influenced by the myriad of interactions, conflicts and developments within that society. Therefore, to analyse the law effectively, one should always consider the broader context in which it operates. This perspective, therefore, requires shifting the focus from a purely doctrinal interpretation of legal instruments and arbitral awards to an understanding of law that encompasses social, economic and political dimensions. When applying this contextual approach to investment arbitration, it becomes evident that the role of investment arbitrators is almost as much about law- and policy-making as it is about the settlement of disputes. As it has been seen, the decisions made by arbitrators do not merely resolve individual disputes: they also contribute to the shaping of international investment law and especially practice. Therefore, one could argue that arbitrators have a series of duties that extend beyond those explicitly

---

1 Vargiu, 'Stakeholders of Investment Arbitration: establishing a dialogue among arbitrators, states, investors, academics and other actors in international investment law', *supra*, Chapter 1, note 1, 15.

specified in the applicable treaties and laws. Indeed, investment arbitration inherently involves considerations that go beyond the immediate legal issues presented by the parties. The outcomes of these arbitrations can influence investment flows, affect national regulatory policies and impact the overall development of international investment law. Given this broader impact, it would be essential to recognise that arbitrators are not just interpreters of the law: they are also actors who participate in the formulation of policies that govern international investment. Their decisions can set precedents, influence state behaviour and shape the expectations of investors and states alike. This *quasi*-policy-making role would entail that arbitrators have a responsibility to consider the broader implications of their decisions and to ensure that their rulings contribute positively to the development of a fair and balanced investment regime.

If one adopts this broader perspective, the duties of investment arbitrators can be seen as encompassing several key responsibilities beyond the narrow confines of legal adjudication. First, arbitrators would have a duty to maintain the legitimacy and integrity of the arbitration process. This involves ensuring that their decisions are not only legally sound but also perceived as fair and just by the parties and the broader international community. Legitimacy is crucial for the acceptance and effectiveness of the arbitration process, and it requires arbitrators to be mindful of the procedural and substantive fairness of their rulings. This duty may sometimes necessitate going beyond the letter of the law to consider principles of equity and justice. Second, arbitrators would have a duty to consider the impact of their decisions on the regulatory autonomy of states. Investment arbitration often involves claims that challenge state regulations, particularly in areas such as environmental protection, public health and labour standards. Arbitrators should therefore balance the protection of investor rights with the need to preserve states' ability to regulate in the public interest. This requires understanding the policy objectives underlying state regulations, and a careful consideration of how arbitration awards might affect those objectives. Arbitrators should strive to avoid decisions that unduly constrain host states' regulatory powers, or that create a chilling effect on legitimate regulatory activities. Third, arbitrators would have a duty to promote coherence and consistency in international investment law. The fragmented nature of the investment regime, characterised by a multitude of bilateral and regional treaties with varying provisions, poses a challenge to the development of a coherent body of law. Arbitrators can certainly contribute to greater coherence by considering past decisions and aiming for consistency in their rulings. While each case is unique, and there is no formal system of binding precedent in international arbitration, consistent and reasoned decision-making can help build a more predictable and stable investment regime. This, in turn, would enhance the confidence of both investors and host states in the system of investment arbitration.

Fourth, and chiefly, arbitrators would have a duty to be aware of and sensitive to the socio-economic and political contexts in which disputes arise. Investment disputes often occur in settings where economic development, social justice and political stability are at stake. Arbitrators should consider how their decisions might affect these broader contexts and strive to render awards that support sustainable development and social progress. Lastly, arbitrators have a duty to engage with (and perhaps contribute to) the broader discourse on the development of international investment law. This involves participating in academic and professional discussions, contributing to the development of best practices, and being open to feedback from the international community. By engaging with the broader legal and policy community, arbitrators can help shape the evolution of investment law in a manner that is responsive to the needs and concerns of all stakeholders.

While recognising the broader contextual approach to the responsibilities of arbitrators has its merits, in my opinion, this perspective extends its duties excessively. This approach rests on two problematic foundations: partially disregarding the applicable law, and implicitly arguing that arbitrators are under a duty to exceed their powers. First, as it has been seen, there is no legal basis within the framework of existing treaties and conventions for arbitrators to assume such expansive roles. The applicable laws, including the ICSID Convention and other arbitration rules, delineate the powers and responsibilities of arbitrators quite clearly. By expecting arbitrators to go beyond these defined boundaries, this approach undermines the legal foundations upon which arbitration is built. Moreover, suggesting that arbitrators have a duty to exceed their powers directly conflicts with the grounds outlined in Article 52 of the ICSID Convention. Article 52(1)(b), as it has been seen, explicitly provides for awards to be annulled if the tribunal has manifestly exceeded its powers. Encouraging arbitrators to interpret their roles in a manner that stretches or exceeds these powers would inevitably lead to numerous annulments of awards. This would not only introduce significant legal uncertainty, but it would also disrupt the sort of reliability that is essential to a credible system of dispute settlement. Moreover, such an approach in practice would paradoxically undermine the very coherence and stability that critics of international investment arbitration seek to enhance. If awards are frequently annulled due to perceived overreach by arbitrators, the trust in the arbitration process would erode even more, and the system's legitimacy would be severely compromised. Rather than achieving a more balanced and fair investment arbitration regime, this approach could lead to greater fragmentation and inconsistency in arbitral awards, further complicating the situation for both investors and host states. Additionally, the suggestion that arbitrators should adopt roles akin to policymakers or social justice advocates places them in positions for which they are neither appointed nor equipped. Arbitrators are selected for their expertise in law and their ability to impartially adjudicate disputes based on the legal frameworks agreed upon by the parties. Expecting them to consider broad socio-economic impacts or to make decisions influenced by policy considerations goes beyond their mandate and intrudes into the domain of state sovereignty and legislative processes.

This approach also risks conflating the distinct roles of arbitrators and judges. While judges in domestic courts might engage in the development of the law within a certain jurisdiction, arbitrators are intended to resolve specific disputes within the parameters set by the parties and the relevant legal instruments. Expanding their remit to include broader policy considerations dilutes their primary function and potentially biases their decisions, thus compromising the neutrality and objectivity that are the hallmarks of effective arbitration.

While the current state of international investment arbitration may not warrant an outright endorsement, acknowledging the flaws within the system is crucial. The scholarship on investment arbitration has increasingly highlighted criticisms concerning the lack of balance in power between foreign investors and host states. This imbalance is not merely a theoretical concern: it is actually becoming more grounded in reality as the system continues to develop. High-profile cases such as *Yukos* and *ConocoPhillips* serve as poignant examples: although these cases are still exceptional, they nonetheless set dangerous precedents that could have far-reaching implications for the entire arbitration framework.[2] Indeed, while these cases may currently be outliers, there is a significant risk that they could pave the way for a normalisation of such large-scale awards. If tribunals increasingly issue awards of this magnitude, they could trigger a cascade of reactions from host states. The financial burden imposed by these mega-awards is likely to prompt states to reconsider their participation in investment treaties, potentially leading to a wave of treaty denunciations.[3] Also, the financial impact of mega-awards on host states cannot be understated. Many states,

2 See *supra*, Chapter 4, notes 13 and 14.

3 See on this point the seminal contributions of Montanes, 'Bolivia's Denunciation of the Convention on the Settlement of Investment Disputes between States and Nationals of Other States', 969–973; Lavopa, Barreiros, and Bruno, 'How to kill a BIT and not die trying: Legal and political challenges of denouncing or renegotiating bilateral investment treaties', 869–891; Kownacki, 'Prospects for ICSID Arbitration

particularly developing countries, may find it challenging to comply with such large financial obligations. The economic strain imposed by mega-awards would divert resources from essential public services and development projects, exacerbating socio-economic inequalities. Moreover, the threat of such substantial financial liabilities could deter states from implementing necessary regulatory measures, particularly in areas such as environmental protection, public health and labour standards. Furthermore, the risk of mega-awards could lead to a chilling effect on foreign investment. If states begin to perceive the system of investment arbitration system as a significant financial risk, they will be less inclined to open their economies to foreign investors or sign new investment agreements. This could reduce the overall flow of foreign investment, which is often crucial for economic development and growth. The resulting reduction in investment could hamper global economic integration and development, particularly in regions that rely heavily on foreign capital. Moreover, the potential collapse of the investment arbitration system due to treaty denunciations poses a significant threat to the stability of international investment relations. The current system, despite its flaws, provides a structured and mostly predictable framework for resolving disputes. If states increasingly withdraw from investment treaties, the resulting *vacuum* could lead to increased uncertainty and conflict in international investment relations. Investors may face greater risks and uncertainties, leading to a decline in cross-border investments and economic cooperation.

While these are all undeniably legitimate and pressing concerns, addressing these issues should not fall within the remit of arbitrators. Arbitrators are tasked with applying the applicable law – that is, BITs and free trade agreements – as it stands. If substantive change is desired, it is the applicable law itself that must be reformed. This principle is a cornerstone of public international law, which maintains that legal frameworks and the duties of adjudicators and arbitrators should be clearly defined and adhered to. Therefore expecting arbitrators to undertake the balancing of powers and interests that extend beyond their mandated responsibilities is both unreasonable and – as I argued above – counterproductive. Asking arbitrators to go beyond their defined role and engage in balancing broader socio-economic or political interests would not only exceed their mandate but also undermine the integrity of the

in Post-Denunciation Countries: An Updated Approach', 529–560; Nyombi and Mortimer, 'Rights and obligations in the post investment treaty denunciation period', 46–53; Rodner and Estévez, 'BITs in Pieces: The Effectiveness of ICSID Jurisdiction after the ICSID Convention Has Been Denounced', 437–451; Voon, Mitchell, 'Denunciation, termination and survival: the interplay of treaty law and international investment law', 413–433.

system of investment law and arbitration. The very function of arbitrators as impartial adjudicators would be jeopardised were they required to consider factors beyond the legal merits of the case. Arbitrators must remain neutral and base their decisions solely on the law and evidence presented. Introducing considerations of public policy or socio-economic impacts into their decision-making process could lead to rather well-founded accusations of bias and partiality, further eroding the already precarious trust in the system. It is therefore essential to preserve the clear distinction between the roles of arbitrators, lawmakers and policymakers to maintain the legitimacy and fairness of the system.

Reforming the applicable law to address these pressing concerns requires a coordinated effort at the level of treaty negotiation and amendment. States must take the lead in rebalancing the rights and obligations within BITs and FTAs to ensure that they adequately protect public interests while providing fair and equitable treatment to investors. This may involve, as it is happening with the UNCITRAL Working Group III, incorporating clearer provisions on regulatory autonomy, introducing mechanisms for greater transparency and public participation, and establishing balanced dispute resolution procedures that reflect the interests of all stakeholders. In addition to treaty reform, though, there evidently is a need for ongoing dialogue and cooperation between states, investors and other stakeholders to develop a more sustainable and equitable investment regime.

Ultimately, the role of arbitrators must remain within the boundaries set by the applicable law. It is through the law that their mandate is defined, and it is through legal reform that the concerns surrounding investment arbitration can be most effectively addressed. Expecting arbitrators to take on responsibilities that extend beyond their legal remit not only undermines the arbitration process but also diverts attention from the necessary reforms at the treaty level.

BIBLIOGRAPHY

Adam Samuel, "The US Supreme Court does Kompetenz-Kompetenz", *Arbitration International* 35(2), 263–273 (2019).

Agata Ferreira, "Intertwined paths of globalization and international investment law", *Journal of International Trade Law and Policy* 19(2), 85–99 (2020).

Alberto Malatesta, "Confidentiality in international commercial arbitration", in Alberto Malatesta, Rinaldo Sali (eds.), *The Rise of Transparency in International Arbitration*, Juris Publishing, 2013, pp. 39–51.

Aldo Zammit Borda, "The use of precedent as subsidiary means and sources of international criminal law", *Tilburg Law Review* 18(2), 65–82 (2013).

Alec Stone Sweet, Florian Grisel, *The Evolution of International Arbitration: Judicialization, Governance, Legitimacy*, Oxford University Press, 2017.

Alec Stone Sweet, Michael Y. Chung, Adam Saltzman, "Arbitral lawmaking and state power: An empirical analysis of investor–state arbitration", *Journal of International Dispute Settlement* 8(4), 579–609 (2017).

Alessandro Monti, Matteo Fermeglia, "The FET Standard between Treaty Reform and ISDS Practice: An Analysis of the Modernized ECT" *Journal of International Arbitration* 41(2), 155–178 (2024).

Alex Grabowski, "The Definition of Investment under the ICSID Convention: A Defense of Salini", *Chicago Journal of International Law* 15(1), 287–309 (2014).

Alexander J. Bělohlávek, "Confidentiality and Publicity in Investment Arbitration, Public Interest and Scope of Powers Vested in Arbitral Tribunals", *Czech Yearbook of International Law* 2, 23–45 (2011).

Alexander J. Bělohlávek, Naděžda Rozehnalová, Filip Černý, *Independence and Impartiality of Arbitrators*, Juris Publishing, 2014.

Alexandra Diehl, *The Core Standard of International Investment Protection: Fair and Equitable Treatment*, Kluwer Law International, 2012.

Alexandre Marques da Silva Martins, "Challenges to transparency and ethics in alternatives to arbitration in the realm of international investments", *Revista de Direito Internacional Econômico e Tributário* 11(1), 321–376 (2016).

Alexis Mourre, "Soft law as a condition for the development of trust in international arbitration", *Revista Brasileira de Arbitragem* 13(51), 82–98 (2016).

Alfred Siwy, "Contract Claims and Treaty Claims", in Crina Baltag (ed.), *ICSID Convention after 50 Years: Unsettled Issues*, Wolters Kluwer, pp. 209–255.

Alvaro Oleart, *Framing TTIP in the European public spheres: towards an empowering dissensus for EU integration*, Palgrave Macmillan, 2021.

Ana Maria Daza-Clark, *International investment law and water resources management: an appraisal of indirect expropriation*, Brill Nijhoff, 2017.

Anders Nilsson, Oscar Englesson, "Inconsistent awards in investment treaty arbitration: is an appeals court needed?", *Journal of International Arbitration* 30(5), 561–579 (2013).

Andrea Giardina, "International investment arbitration: recent developments as to the applicable law and unilateral recourse", *The Law and Practice of International Courts and Tribunals* 5(1), 29–39 (2006).

Andrea J. Menaker, Eckhard R. Hellbeck, "Piercing the Veil of Confidentiality: the Recent Trend towards Greater Public Participation and Transparency in Investment Treaty Arbitration", in Katia Yannaca-Small (ed.), *Arbitration Under International Investment Agreements – A Guide to the Key Issues*, Oxford University Press, 2018, pp. 183–219.

Andrea K. Bjorklund, "Are arbitrators (judicial) activists?", *Law & Practice of International Courts & Tribunals* 17(1), 49–60 (2018).

Andrea K. Bjorklund, "The Legitimacy of the International Centre for Settlement of Investment Disputes", in Nienke Grossman, Harlan Grant Cohen, Andreas Follesdal, Geir Ulfstein (eds.), *Legitimacy and International Courts*, Cambridge University Press, 2018, pp. 234–283.

Andrea K. Bjorklund, Daniel Behn, Susan D. Franck, Chiara Giorgetti, Won Kidane, Arnaud de Nanteuil, Emilia Onyema, "The diversity deficit in international investment arbitration", *The Journal of World Investment & Trade* 21(2–3), 410–440 (2020).

Andreas Kulick (ed.), *Reassertion of control over the investment treaty regime*, Cambridge University Press, 2017.

Andrew Byrnes, Mika Hayashi, Christopher Michaelsen, *International law in the new age of globalization*, Martinus Nijhoff Publishers, 2013.

Andrew Paul Newcombe, Lluís Paradell, *Law and Practice f Investment Treaties: Standards of Treatment*, Wolters Kluwer, 2009.

Angelina M. Petti, Nathalie Voser, "The revised IBA guidelines on conflicts of interest in international arbitration", *ASA Bulletin* 33(1), 6–36 (2015).

Anil Yilmaz Vastardis, Gus Van Harten, "Critiques of investment arbitration reform: an introduction", *The Journal of World Investment and Trade* 24(3), 363–371 (2023).

Anne van Aaken, "Primary and Secondary Remedies in International Investment Law and National State Liability – A Functional and Comparative View", in Stephan W. Schill (ed.), International Investment Law and Public Law, Oxford University Press 2010, p. 722.

Antoine Martin, "Definition of "Investment": Could a Persistent Objector to the Salini Tests be Found in ICSID Arbitral Practice?", *Global Jurist* 11(2), Article 3, pp. 20122005 (2023).

Antonio Parra, "Applicable Law in Investor-State Arbitration", in Michael Rovine (ed.), *Contemporary Issues in International Arbitration and Mediation: The Fordham Papers*, Vol. I, Martinus Nijhoff, 2008.

Antonio Parra, *The History of ICSID*, Oxford University Press, 2012.

Arman Sarvarian, Rudy Baker, Filippo Fontanelli and Vassilis Tsevelekos (eds.), *Procedural fairness in international courts and tribunals*, British Institute of International and Comparative Law, 2015.

Arnaud de Nanteuil, "Expropriation", in Makane M. Mbengue, Stefanie Schacherer (eds.), *Foreign Investment Under the Comprehensive Economic and Trade Agreement (CETA). Studies in European Economic Law and Regulation*, Vol. 15. Springer, 2019.

Asif Qureshi, "An appellate system in international investment arbitration?", in *Peter Muchlinski, Federico Ortino, Christoph Schreuer, The Oxford Handbook of International Investment Law*, Oxford University Press, 2008, p. 1154.

Attila Tanzi, "On judicial autonomy and the autonomy of the parties in international adjudication, with special regard to investment arbitration and ICSID annulment proceedings", *Leiden Journal of International Law* 33(1), 57–75 (2020).

August Reinisch (ed.), *Standards of investment protection*, Oxford University Press, 2008.

August Reinisch, "Investment Arbitration and the Rule of Law", in Stefan Kröll, Andrea K. Bjorklund, Franco Ferrari, *Cambridge Compendium of International Commercial and Investment Arbitration*, Cambridge University Press, 2023, pp. 211–243.

August Reinisch, "National Treatment", in Marc Bungenberg, Jörn Griebel, Stephan Hobe, August Reinisch (eds.), *International Investment Law: A Handbook*, C.H. Beck/Hart/Nomos, 2015, pp. 846–869.

August Reinisch, Christoph Schreuer, *International protection of investments: the substantive standards*, Cambridge University Press, 2020.

August Reinisch, Stephan Schill (eds.), *Investment protection standards and the rule of law*, Oxford University Press, 2023.

Barton Legum, "Options to establish an Appellate Mechanism for Investment Disputes", in Karl Sauvant, (ed.), *Appeals Mechanism in International Investment Disputes*, Oxford University Press (2008), pp. 231–240.

Berk Demirkol, "Non-treaty claims in investment treaty arbitration", *Leiden Journal of International Law* 31(1), 59–91 (2018).

Biriş Bogdan Ovidiu, "Advantages and disadvantages of transparency and public participation in investment arbitration", *Revista Romana de Arbitraj* 12(1), 16–27 (2018).

Campbell McLachlan, Laurence Shore, Matthew Weiniger, *International Investment Arbitration: Substantive Principles*, Oxford University Press, 2017.

Carl Bruch, Carroll Muffett and Sandra S. Nichols (Eds.), *Governance, natural resources and post-conflict peacebuilding*, Earthscan, 2016.

Carlo De Stefano, "From arbitrators to judges? reflections on the reform of investor-state dispute settlement", *Italian Yearbook of International Law* 29, 137–161 (2019).

Carlos Esplugues Mota, *Foreign investment and investment arbitration in Asia*, Intersentia, (2019).

Carlos Ignacio Suarez Anzorena, "Vivendi v. Argentina: on the Admissibility of Requests for Partial Annulment and the Ground of Manifest Excess of Powers", in Emmanuel Gaillard and Yas Banifatemi, *Annulment of ICSID Awards – A Joint IAI–ASIL Conference Washington, D.C. – April 1, 2003*, Juris Publishing, 2004, pp. 123–175.

Catharine Titi, "The arbitrator as a lawmaker: Jurisgenerative processes in investment arbitration", *The Journal of World Investment & Trade* 14(5), 829–851 (2013).

Catherine A. Rogers, "The vocation of the international arbitrator", *American University International Law Review* 20(5), 957–1020 (2005).

Cecilia Carrara, "Conflicts of interests", *Journal of International Arbitration* 39(3), 379–396 (2022).

Chiara Giorgetti, "Arbitrator Challenges in International Investment Tribunals", in Daniel Behn, Ole Kristian Fauchald, Malcolm Langford (eds.), *The Legitimacy of Investment Arbitration: Empirical Perspectives*, Cambridge University Press, 2022, pp. 133–158.

Chiara Giorgetti, "Between legitimacy and control: challenges and recusals of judges and arbitrators in international courts and tribunals", *George Washington International Law Review* 49(2), 205–258 (2016).

Chiara Giorgetti, "Who decides who decides in international investment arbitration", *University of Pennsylvania Journal of International Law* 35(3), 431–486 (2014).

Chiara Giorgetti, *Challenges and recusals of judges and arbitrators in international courts and tribunals*, Brill Nijhoff, 2015.

Chittharanjan Amerasinghe, *International Arbitral Jurisdiction*, Martinus Nijhoff, 2011.

Chrispas Nyombi, Tom Mortimer, "Rights and obligations in the post investment treaty denunciation period", *International Arbitration Law Review* 21(2), 46–53 (2018).

Christian Riffel, "Indirect expropriation and the protection of public interests", *International and Comparative Law Quarterly* 71(4), 945–974 (2022).

Christian Tams, "An appealing option? the debate about an ICSID appellate structure", *Essays in Transnational Economic Law No.* 57 (2006), p. 14.

Christina Knahr, August Reinisch, "Transparency versus Confidentiality in International Investment Arbitration – The Biwater Gauff Compromise", *The Law and Practice of International Courts and Tribunals* 6(1), 97–118 (2007).

Christina L. Beharry, Elisa Méndez Bräutigam, "Damages and valuation in international investment arbitration", in Julien Chaisse, Leïla Choukroune, Sufian Jusoh (eds.), *Handbook of International Investment Law and Policy*, Springer, 2020, pp. 1423–1454.

Christoph Schreuer, "Consent to Arbitration", in *Peter Muchlinski, Federico Ortino, Christoph Schreuer, The Oxford Handbook of International Investment Law*, Oxford University Press, 2008, p. 830.

Christoph Schreuer, "ICSID Annulment Revisited", *Legal Issues of Economic Integration* 30, 103–122 (2003).

Christoph Schreuer, "Investment Treaty Arbitration and Jurisdiction over Contract Claims: the Vivendi I Case considered", in Todd Weiler (ed.), *International investment law and arbitration: leading cases from the ICSID, NAFTA, bilateral treaties and customary international law*, Cameron May, 2005, pp. 281–323.

Christoph Schreuer, "Jurisdiction and Applicable Law in Investment Treaty Arbitration", *McGill Journal of Dispute Resolution* 1(1), 1–25 (2014).

Christoph Schreuer, Loretta Malintoppi, August Reinisch, Anthony Sinclair, *The ICSID Convention: a commentary*, Cambridge University Press, 2010.

Christoph Schreuer, "Víctor Pey Casado and President Allende Foundation v Republic of Chile: Barely an Annulment", *ICSID Review – Foreign Investment Law Journal* 29, 321–327 (2014).

Claire Cutler, David Lark, "The hidden costs of law in the governance of global supply chains: the turn to arbitration", *Review of International Political Economy* 29(3), 719–748 (2022).

Crina Baltag, Ana Stanič (eds.), *The future of investment treaty arbitration in the EU intra-EU BITs, the Energy Charter Treaty, and the Multilateral Investment Court*, Kluwer Law International, 2020.

Damien Charlotin, "The place of investment awards and WTO decisions in international law: a citation analysis", *Journal of International Economic Law* 20(2), 279–299 (2017).

Daniel Behn, Malcolm Langford, Laura Létourneau-Tremblay, "Empirical perspectives on investment arbitration: what do we know? Does it matter?", *The Journal of World Investment and Trade* 21(2), 188–250 (2020).

Daphna Kapeliuk, "Dissents in Investment Arbitration: On Collegiality and Individualism", in Daniel Behn, Ole Kristian Fauchald, Malcolm Langford (eds.), *The Legitimacy of Investment Arbitration: Empirical Perspectives*, Cambridge University Press, 2022, pp. 159–168.

Daphna Kapeliuk, "The repeat appointment factor: exploring decision patterns of elite investment arbitrators", *Cornell Law Review* 96(2), 47–90 (2011).

Darius Chan, Justin Lai, "Two decades after Salini v Morocco: the case for retaining the Salini test with modifications", *Arbitration International* 39(1), 63–84 (2023).

David Caron, "Reputation and Reality in the ICSID Annulment Process: Understanding the Distinction Between Annulment and Appeal", *ICSID Review – Foreign Investment Law Journal* 7, 21–56 (1992).

David Schneiderman, "Legitimacy and Reflexivity in International Investment Arbitration: A New Self-Restraint?", *Journal of International Dispute Settlement* 2(2), 471–495 (2011).

David Soto Díaz, *El árbitro en el sistema CIADI: estudio acerca de la independencia, imparcialidad, deberes, derechos y responsabilidad de los árbitros CIADI*, Tirant lo Blanch, 2020.

Debora Visconte, "Competência Arbitral. Princípio Kompetenz-Kompetenz. Alegação de Contrato de Adesão", *Revista Brasileira de Arbitragem* 35(9), 93–109 (2012).

Dima Jamali, Charlotte Karam, "Corporate social responsibility in developing countries as an emerging field of study", *International Journal of Management Reviews* 20(1), 32–61 (2018).

Dinah Shelton, *Remedies in International Human Rights Law*, Oxford University Press, 1999.

Dolores Bentolila, *Arbitrators as Lawmakers*, Kluwer Law International (2017).

Donald McRae, "The WTO Appellate Body: A Model for an ICSID Appeals Facility?", *Journal of International Dispute Settlement* 1(2), 371–387 (2010).

Eckhard Janeba, "Regulatory chill and the effect of investor state dispute settlements", *Review of International Economics* 27(4), 1172–1198 (2019).

Elza Reymond-Eniaeva (ed.), *Towards a uniform approach to confidentiality of international commercial arbitration*, Springer, 2019.

Emilie M. Hafner-Burton, Zachary C. Steinert-Threlkeld, David G. Victor, "Predictability Versus Flexibility: Secrecy in International Investment Arbitration", *World Politics* 68(3), 413–453 (2016).

Emily Sipiorski, *Good faith in international investment arbitration*, Oxford University Press, 2019.

Emmanuel Gaillard, "Sociology of international arbitration", *Arbitration International* 31(1), 1–17 (2015).

Emmanuel Gaillard, Yas Banifatemi, "The Meaning of "and" in Article 42(1), Second Sentence, of the Washington Convention: The Role of International Law in the ICSID Choice of Law Process", *ICSID Review – Foreign Investment Law Journal* 18, 375–411 (2003).

Eric De Brabandere, "Arbitral Decisions As a Source of International Investment Law", in Tarcisio Gazzini, Eric De Brabandere (eds.), *International Investment Law – The Sources of Rights and Obligations*, Brill Nijhoff, 2012, pp. 245–288.

Eric De Brabandere, *Investment treaty arbitration as public international law: procedural aspects and implications,* Cambridge University Press, 2016.

Ernst-Ulrich Petersmann, "The judicial task of administering justice in trade and investment law and adjudication", *Journal of International Dispute Settlement* 4(1), 5–28 (2013).

Fabien Gélinas, "The Independence of International Arbitrators and Judges: Tampered with or Well Tempered?", *New York International Law Review* 24(1), 1–48 (2011).

Fabio Morosini, Michelle Ratton Sanchez Badin (eds.), *Reconceptualizing international investment law from the global south*, Cambridge University Press, 2017.

Fali S. Nariman, "Standards of Behaviour of Arbitrators", *Arbitration International* 4(4), 311–321 (1988).

Farouk Yala, "The Notion of "Investment" in ICSID Case Law: a Drifting Jurisdictional Requirement? Some "Un-Conventional" Thoughts on Salini, SGS and Mihaly", *Journal of International Arbitration* 22(2), 105–126 (2005).

Federico M. Lavopa, Lucas E. Barreiros, M. Victoria Bruno, "How to kill a BIT and not die trying: Legal and political challenges of denouncing or renegotiating bilateral investment treaties", *Journal of International Economic Law* 16(4), 869–891 (2013).

Felix Dasser, *"Soft law" in international commercial arbitration*, Brill Nijhoff, 2021.

Ferdi de Ville, Gabriel Siles-Brügge, *T.T.I.P. : the truth about the transatlantic trade and investment partnership*, Polity Press, 2016.

Fernando Dias Simões, "Investment Arbitration and the Chimera of an Ideal Adjudicative Community", *Journal of World Investment & Trade* 22(5), 687–704 (2021).

Fernando Loureiro Bastos, "A Southern African Approach to the Permanent Sovereignty over Natural Resources and Common Resource Management Systems", in Marc Bungenberg, Stephan Hobe (eds.), *Permanent Sovereignty over Natural Resources*, Springer, 2015, pp. 61–78.

Fernando Tupa, *The dilemma of consent to international arbitration in investment agreements without a forum*, Brill Nijhoff, 2023.

Flavia Marisi, "Independence and Impartiality: the Role of Soft Law in International Arbitration", *Arbitration: the journal of the Chartered Institute of Arbitrators*, 85(4), 326–345 (2019).

Francesca Romanin Jacur, Angelica Bonfanti, Francesco Seatzu, *Natural resources grabbing: an international law perspective*, Brill Nijhoff, 2016.

Francisco Blavi, "A Case in Favour of Publicity Available Awards in International Commercial Arbitration: Transparency v. Confidentiality", *Revue de droit des affaires internationals* 1(2016), 83–92 (2016).

Frank J. Garcia, Brooke S. Guven, "Designing a Multilateral Investment Court for Procedural Justice", *The Journal of World Investment & Trade* 24(3), 461–486 (2023).

Frédéric Mégret, "International Judges and Experts' Impartiality and the Problem of Past Declarations", *The Law and Practice of International Courts and Tribunals* 10(1), 31–66 (2011).

Friedrich Rosenfeld, "The Hardening of Soft Law in International Arbitration", *European International Arbitration Review* 7(2), 19–36 (2018).

Fulvio Maria Palombino, *Fair and equitable treatment and the fabric of general principles*, Springer, 2018.

Gabriel Bottini, Catharine Titi, Facundo Pérez Aznar, Julien Chaisse, Marko Jovanovic, Olga Puigdemont Sola, "Excessive Costs and Recoverability of Costs Awards in Investment Arbitration", *The Journal of World Investment & Trade* 21(2–3), 251–299 (2020).

Gabrielle Kaufmann-Kohler, "Arbitral Precedent: Dream, Necessity or Excuse – The 2006 Freshfields Lecture", *Arbitration International* 23(3), 357–378 (2007).

Gabrielle Kaufmann-Kohler, Michele Potestà, "Why Investment Arbitration and Not Domestic Courts? The Origins of the Modern Investment Dispute Resolution System, Criticism, and Future Outlook", in Gabrielle Kaufmann-Kohler, Michele Potestà (eds.), *Investor-State Dispute Settlement and National Courts. European Yearbook of International Economic Law*, Springer, 2020, pp. 7–29.

Gabrielle Kaufmann-Kohler, Michele Potestà, *The Composition of a Multilateral Investment Court and of an Appeal Mechanism for Investment Awards*, CIDS, 2017.

Gary Born, *International Commercial Arbitration*, Kluwer Law International, 2021.

Georgios I. Zekos, *Judges and Arbitrators as Law Makers. Advanced Artificial Intelligence and Robo-Justice*, Springer, 2022.

Gilles Cuniberti, *The UNCITRAL Model Law on International Commercial Arbitration: a commentary*, Edward Elgar, 2022.

Giovanni Zarra, "Applicable Law in Investment Arbitration: the 2021 Practice", *The Italian Yearbook of International Law* 31, 391–420 (2021).

Giuditta Cordero-Moss, *International commercial contracts: contract terms, applicable law and arbitration*, Cambridge University Press, 2024.

Giuditta Cordero-Moss, "Tribunal's Power versus Party Autonomy", in *Peter Muchlinski, Federico Ortino, Christoph Schreuer, The Oxford Handbook of International Investment Law*, Oxford University Press, 2008, p. 1207.

Gracious Avayiwoe, "Ensuring North-South Diversity in and Legitimacy of International Investment Arbitration: Africa in Perspective", June 30, 2021.

Gus Van Harten, "Arbitrator Behaviour in Asymmetrical Adjudication: An Empirical Study of Investment Treaty Arbitration", *Oosgode Hall Law Journal* 50(2), 211–268 (2012).

Gus Van Harten, "Leaders in the Expansive and Restrictive Interpretation of Investment Treaties: A Descriptive Study of ISDS Awards to 2010", *European Journal of International Law* 29(2), 507–549 (2018).

Hanno Wehland, "Setting-Aside Proceedings Against Treaty-Based Arbitral Awards in Switzerland and Their Contribution to the Debate Regarding the Fundamental Requirements for Protection under Investment Treaties", *Journal of International Arbitration* 41(5), 559–576 (2024).

Hans Smit, Vratislav Pěchota, *International commercial arbitration and the courts*, Juris Publishing, 2004.

Hans van Houtte, Maurizio Brunetti, "Investment arbitration – ten areas of caution for commercial arbitrators", *Arbitration International* 29(4), 553–574 (2013).

Harlan Grant Cohen, Andreas Follesdal, Nienke Grossman, Geir Ulfstein, *Legitimacy and international courts*, Cambridge University Press, 2018.

Hege Elisabeth Kjos, *Applicable law in investor-state arbitration: the interplay between national and international law*, Oxford University Press, 2013.

Hélène Ruiz Fabri, Edoardo Stoppioni (eds.), *International Investment Law – An Analysis of the Major Decisions*, Hart Publishing, 2022.

Herbert Kronke, Patricia Nacimiento, Dirk Otto, Nicola Christine Port (eds.), *Recognition and Enforcement of Foreign Arbitral Awards: A Global Commentary on the New York Convention*, Kluwer Law International, 2010, pp. 205–344.

Ignacio Torterola, Farhod Sharipov, "The 2022 ICSID Arbitration Rules: Modernizing International Investment Dispute Resolution", *ICSID Review – Foreign Investment Law Journal* 39(1), 52–60 (2024).

Ileana M. Smeureanu, *Confidentiality in international commercial arbitration*, Kluwer Law International, 2011.

Ina C. Popova, Katherine R. Seifert, "Gatekeeping, Lawmaking, and Rulemaking: Lessons from Third-Party Funding in Investment Arbitration", in Katia Katia Fach Gómez (ed.), *Private Actors in International Investment Law*, Springer, 2021, pp. 133–155.

Ingrid A. Müller, "Iura Novit Curia versus Iura Novit Arbiter in International Arbitration", *International Investment Law Journal* 2(2), 137–142 (2022).

Ioana Tudor, *The fair and equitable treatment standard in the international law of foreign investment*, Oxford University Press, 2008.

Irmgard Marboe, "Compensation and Damages in International Law", *Journal of World Investment and Trade* 7(5), 723–759 (2006).

Irmgard Marboe, *Calculation of Compensation and Damages in International Investment Law*, Oxford University Press, 2009, pp. 153 ff.

J. Benton Heath, "Investment Arbitration and State-Driven Reform: New Treaties, Old Outcomes", ICSID Review – Foreign Investment Law *Journal* 38(3), 717–721 (2024).

Jacomijn van Haersolte-van Hof, "Impartiality and independence: fundamental and fluid", *Arbitration International* 37(3), 599–611 (2021).

James Boyd White, *The Legal Imagination*, University of Chicago Press, 1973.

James Devaney, "Selecting Investment Arbitrators: Reconciling Party Autonomy and the International Rule of Law", *KFG Working Paper Series, No. 33, Berlin Potsdam Research Group "The International Rule of Law – Rise or Decline?"*, Berlin, May 2019.

James O. Rodner, Jaime Martínez Estévez, "BITs in Pieces: The Effectiveness of ICSID Jurisdiction after the ICSID Convention Has Been Denounced", *Journal of International Arbitration* 29(4), 437–451 (2012).

Jarrod Hepburn, Martins Paparinskis, Lauge N. Poulsen, Michael Waibel, "Investment law before arbitration", *Journal of International Economic Law* 23(4), 929–947 (2020).

Jason Clapham, "Finality of investor-state arbitral awards: has the tide turned and is there a need for reform?", *Journal of International Arbitration* 26(3), 437–466 (2009).

Jean-Frédéric Morin (ed.), *The politics of transatlantic trade negotiations: TTIP in a globalized world*, Ashgate, 2015.

Jeffery Commission, Rahim Moloo, *Procedural Issues in International Investment Arbitration*, Oxford University Press, 2018.

Jeswald W. Salacuse, "The emerging global regime for investment", *Harvard International Law Journal* 51(2), 427–473 (2010).

Jeswald W. Salacuse, *The Law of Investment Treaties*, Oxford University Press, 2021.

Jeswald W. Salacuse, *The three laws of international investment: national, contractual, and international frameworks for foreign capital*, Oxford University Press, 2013.

Jill I. Gross, "Arbitration Archetypes for Enhancing Access to Justice", *Fordham Law Review* 88(6), 2319–2336 (2020).

Jimmy Skjold Hansen, ""Missing Links" in Investment Arbitration: Quantification of Damages to Foreign Shareholders", *The Journal of World Investment & Trade* 14(3), 434–479 (2013).

Joanna Lam, "Legal interpretation and adjudicatory activism in international commercial arbitration", in Anne Lise Kjaer, Joanna Lam, (eds.). *Language and Legal Interpretation in International Law*, Oxford University Press, 2022, pp. 236–255.

Joel Dahlquist and Kaj Hober, *Investment Treaty Arbitration: Problems and Exercises*, Edward Elgar Publishing, 2018.

Johan Eliasson, Patricia García-Durán Huet, *Civil society, rhetoric of resistance, and transatlantic trade*, Palgrave Macmillan, 2019.

John J. Barceló III, "The Competence-Competence Principle's Negative Effect", in Stefan Kröll, Andrea K. Bjorklund, Franco Ferrari (eds.), *Cambridge Compendium of International Commercial and Investment Arbitration*, Cambridge University Press, 2023, pp 807–847.

John R. Crook, "Applicable Law in International Arbitration: The Iran-U.S. Claims Tribunal Experience", *American Journal of International Law* 83(2), 278–311 (1989).

John William Rowley, Emmanuel Gaillard, Gordon E. Kaiser, Benjamin Siino (eds.), *The guide to challenging and enforcing arbitration awards, GAR – Law Business Research*, 2021.

John Y. Gotanda, "Consistently Inconsistent: The Need for Predictability in Awarding Costs and Fees in Investment Treaty Arbitrations", ICSID Review – Foreign Investment Law *Journal* 28(2), 420–437 (2013).

Jonathan Bonnitcha, Lauge N. Poulsen, Michael Waibel, *The political economy of the investment treaty regime*, Oxford University Press, 2017.

Jonathan Cowe, "'It's not me, it's you': Arbitrator's Conduct and the Public's Opinion of ISDS", *Arbitration* 85(3), 251–262 (2019).

Jonathan Hill, "Claims that an arbitral tribunal failed to deal with an issue: the setting aside of awards under the Arbitration Act 1996 and the UNCITRAL Model Law on International Commercial Arbitration", *Arbitration International* 34(3), 385–414 (2018).

Jorge Alberto Huerta-Goldman, Antoine Romanetti, Franz Stirnimann (eds.), *WTO litigation, investment arbitration, and commercial arbitration*, Kluwer Law International, 2013.

José E. Álvarez, "Reviewing the Use of "Soft Law" in Investment Arbitration", *European International Arbitration Review* 7(2), 149–200 (2018).

José Manuel Álvarez Zárate, "Nineteenth Century Arbitrators' Powers – Has There Been Any Progress to Date?", *Law & Practice of International Courts & Tribunals* 17(1), 217–235 (2018).

Joshua Fellenbaum, "Putting the Needle to the Salini Bubble?", in Todd Weiler (ed.), *Investment treaty arbitration and international law*, Vol. 5, JurisNet, 2012, pp. 103–151.

Julian Donaubauer, Eric Neumayer, Peter Nunnenkamp, "Winning or losing in investor-to-state dispute resolution: the role of arbitrator bias and experience", *Review of International Economics* 26(4), 892–916 (2018).

Julian Scheu, Lisa Schöttmer (eds.), *Creation and implementation of a multilateral investment court*, Nomos, 2022.

Julien Fouret, "Denunciation of the Washington Convention and Non-Contractual Investment Arbitration: "Manufacturing Consent" to ICSID Arbitration?", *Journal of International Arbitration* 25(1), 71–87 (2008).

Karl Sauvant, José E. Alvarez (eds.), *The evolving international investment regime: expectations, realities, options*, Oxford University Press, 2011.

Karl-Heinz Böckstiegel, "Commercial and investment arbitration: how different are they today?: The Lalive lecture", *Arbitration International* 28(4), 577–590 (2012).

Katia Fach Gómez, *Key Duties of International Investment Arbitrators: a Transnational Study of Legal and Ethical Dilemmas*, Springer, 2019.

Kenneth J Vandevelde, *The first bilateral investment treaties: U.S. postwar friendship, commerce, and navigation treaties*, Oxford University Press, 2017.

Kenneth S. Jacob, "Reinvigorating ICSID With a New Mission and With Renewed Respect for Party Autonomy", *Virginia Journal of International Law* 33, 123–160 (1992).

Kevin Tan, Michael Hwang, "The Time Limit to Set Aside an Award Under Article 34(3) of the Model Law: A Comparative Study", *Journal of International Arbitration* 38(5), 553–600 (2021).

Ksenia Polonskaya, "Diversity in the investor-state arbitration: Intersectionality must be a part of the conversation", *Melbourne Journal of International Law* 19(1), 259–298 (2018).

Kyla Tienhaara, "Regulatory chill in a warming world: The threat to climate policy posed by Investor-State Dispute Settlement", *Transnational Environmental Law* 7(2), 229–250 (2018).

Lars Markert, "Improving Efficiency in Investment Arbitration", *Contemporary Asia Arbitration Journal* 4(2), 215–246 (2011).

Lauge S. Poulsen, The Significance of South-South BITs for the International Investment Regime: A Quantitative Analysis, *Northwestern Journal of International Law and Business* 30(1), 101–130 (2009).

Laurence Boisson de Chazournes, "Plurality in the Fabric of International Courts and Tribunals: The Threads of a Managerial Approach", *European Journal of International Law* 28(1), 13–72 (2017).

Laurence Burger, "The Trouble with Salini (Criticism of and Alternatives to the Famous Test)", *ASA Bulletin* 31(3), 521–536 (2013).

Laurens Timmer, "Manifest Excess of Powers as a Ground for the Annulment of ICSID Awards", *Journal of World Investment & Trade* 14(5), 775–803 (2013).

Lawrence W. Newman, Michael J. Radine (eds.), *Soft law in international arbitration*, Juris Publishing, 2014.

Leila Choukroune, "National Treatment in International Investment Law and Arbitration: A Relative Standard for Autonomous Public Regulation and Sovereign Development", in Anselm Kamperman Sanders (ed.), *The principle of national treatment in international economic law: trade, investment and intellectual property*, Edward Elgar, 2014, pp. 183–219.

Leon E. Trakman, "Confidentiality in international commercial arbitration", *Arbitration International* 18(1), 1–18 (2002).

Lewis B. Kaden, "Judges and Arbitrators: Observations on the Scope of Judicial Review", 80(2) *Columbia Law Review* 80(2), 267–298 (1980).

Lorenzo Cotula, Nicolás M. Perrone, "Seeing Santurbán through ISDS: A sociolegal case study of Eco Oro v. Colombia", *Leiden Journal of International Law* 37(2), 440–461 (2024).

Louis Brennan, *Enacting globalization: multidisciplinary perspectives on international integration*, Palgrave MacMillan, 2014.

Lucas Clover Alcolea, "Arbitral Activism and Choice of Law under the ICSID Convention", *Chinese Journal of International Law* 21(3), 499–546 (2022).

Lucy Greenwood, C. Mark Baker, "Is the balance getting better? An update on the issue of gender diversity in international arbitration", *Arbitration International* 31(3), 413–442 (2015).

Lucy Reed, "The "De Facto" Precedent Regime in Investment Arbitration: a Case for Proactive Case Management", *ICSID review – Foreign Investment Law Journal* 25(1), 95–103 (2010).

Ludovica Chiussi Curzi, ""No matter how egregious" : misapplication of the law and manifest excess of powers in ICSID arbitration", in Giuditta Cordero-Moss and Diego P. Fernández Arroyo, *Applicable law issues in international arbitration – Questions de droit applicable dans l'arbitrage international*, Brill Nijhoff, 2023, pp. 303–323.

Luke Nottage, Nobumichi Teramura and James Tanna, "Developing diversity within diversity discourse: remembering non-lawyers in arbitration", in Shahla F. Ali, Filip Balcerzak, Giorgio Fabio Colombo, Joshua Karton (eds.), *Diversity in International Arbitration – Why it Matters and How to Sustain It*, Edward Elgar, 2022, pp. 101–118.

Magdalene D'Silva, "Dealing in power: gatekeepers in arbitrator appointment in international commercial arbitration", *Journal of International Dispute Settlement* 5(3), 605–634 (2014).

Malcolm Langford, Daniel Behn, "Managing Backlash: The Evolving Investment Treaty Arbitrator?", *European Journal of International Law* 29(2), 551–580 (2018).

Malcolm Langford, Daniel Behn, and Runar Hilleren Lie, "The revolving door in international investment arbitration", *Journal of International Economic Law* 20(2), 301–332 (2017).

Manuel Penadés Fons, Pedro Tent Alonso, "The New York Convention and the Enforcement of Arbitration Agreements by National Courts: What Level of Review?", in Katia Fach Gómez, Ana Mercedes López Rodríguez (eds.), *60 Years of the New York Convention: Key Issues and Future Challenges*, Kluwer Law International, 2019.

Marc Bungenberg, "Democracy and International Investment Law", in Stefan Kröll, Andrea K. Bjorklund, Franco Ferrari (eds.), *Cambridge Compendium of International Commercial and Investment Arbitration*, Cambridge University Press, 2023, pp. 186–210.

Marc Bungenberg, August Reinisch, *Draft Statute of the Multilateral Investment Court*, Nomos, 2021.

Marc Bungenberg, August Reinisch, *From bilateral arbitral tribunals and investment courts to a multilateral investment court: options regarding the institutionalization of investor-state dispute settlement*, Springer, 2020.

Marco Tulio Montanes, "Bolivia's Denunciation of the Convention on the Settlement of Investment Disputes between States and Nationals of Other States", *International Legal Materials* 46(5), 969–973 (2007).

Margaret M. Moses, *The principles and practice of international commercial arbitration*, Cambridge University Press, 2024.

Maria Laura Marceddu, Pietro Ortolani, "What is wrong with investment arbitration? Evidence from a set of behavioural experiments", *European Journal of International Law* 31(2), 405–428 (2020).

Maria Nicole Cleis, *The independence and impartiality of ICSID arbitrators: current case law, alternative approaches, and improvement suggestions*, Brill Nijhoff, 2017.

Mariel Dimsey, Sanjna Pramod, "Selection, Bias, and Ethics of Arbitrators in Investor-State Arbitration", in Julien Chaisse, Leïla Choukroune, Sufian Jusoh (eds.), *Handbook of International Investment Law and Policy*, Springer, 2020, 1–40.

Markus Petsche, "The Application of the Salini Test Beyond Article 25 of the ICSID Convention: Analysis of Recent Trends in Treaty and Arbitral Practice", *The Journal of World Investment & Trade* 24(6), 879–906 (2023).

Markus Petsche, *The concept of investment in ICSID arbitration*, Oxford University Press, 2023.

Marting Paparinskis, "'Crippling compensation in the International Law Commission and investor-state arbitration", ICSID Review – Foreign Investment Law *Journal* 37(1–2), 289–312 (2022).

Martins Paparinskis, "A Case Against Crippling Compensation in International Law of State Responsibility", *Modern Law Review* 83(6), 1246–1286 (2020).

Martins Paparinskis, *The International Minimum Standard and Fair and Equitable Treatment*, Oxford University Press, 2013.

Matthew Hodgson, "Costs in Investment Treaty Arbitration: The Case for Reform", in Jean E. Kalicki, Anna Joubin-Bret (eds.), *Reshaping the investor-state dispute settlement system*, Brill Nijhoff, 2015, pp. 748–759.

Matthew T. Parish, Annalise K. Newlson, Charles B. Rosenberg, "Awarding moral damages to respondent states in investment arbitration", *Berkeley Journal of International Law* 29(1), 225–245 (2011).

Mavluda Sattorova, "Return to the Local Remedies Rule in European BITs? Power (Inequalities), Dispute Settlement, and Change in Investment Treaty Law", *Legal Issues of Economic Integration* 39(2), 223–247 (2012).

Michael Goldhaber, "Wanted: a World Investment Court", 3 Transnational Dispute *Management* (2004).

Michael Waibel, "Putting the MFN Genie Back in the Bottle", *AJIL Unbound* 112, 60–63 (2018).

Michael Waibel, Asha Kaushal, Kyo-Hwa (Liz) Chung, Claire Balchin (eds.), *The Backlash against Investment Arbitration: Perceptions and Reality*, Kluwer Law International, 2010.

Michele Potestà, "Appointment of Arbitrators in the Changing ISDS Landscape", *Swiss Review of International and European Law* 31(2), 231–239 (2021).

Michele Potestà, "Il consenso all'arbitrato ICSID contenuto in una legge nazionale dello stato ospite dell'investimento", *Diritto del Commercio Internazionale* 24(2), 375–396 (2010).

Michele Potestà, "The interpretation of consent to ICSID arbitration contained in domestic investment laws", *Arbitration International* 27(2), 149–169 (2011).

Mohamed Abdel Wahab, "Ascertaining the Content of the Applicable Law in International Arbitration: Converging Civil and Common Law Approaches", *Arbitration: The International Journal of Arbitration, Mediation and Dispute Management* 83(4), 412–422 (2017).

Mojtaba Dani, Afshin Akhtar-Khavari, "The Uncertainty of Legal Doctrine in Indirect Expropriation Cases and the Legitimacy Problems of Investment Arbitration", *Widener Law Review* 22(1), 1–32 (2016).

Monika Florczak-Wątor, *Constitutional Law and Precedent: International Perspectives on Case-Based Reasoning*, Routledge, 2022.

Monique Sasson, "Investment Arbitration: Procedure", in Marc Bungenberg, Jörn Griebel, Stephan Hobe, August Reinisch (eds.), *International Investment Law: A Handbook*, C.H. Beck/Hart/Nomos, 2015, pp. 1288–1372.

Murray L. Smith, "Contractual obligations Owed by and to arbitrators: Model terms of Appointment", *Arbitration International* 8(1), 17–40 (1992).

Murray L. Smith, "Impartiality of the party-appointed arbitrator", *Arbitration International* 6(4), 320–342 (1990).

Mushegh Manukyan, "Hidden in the curtain of Article 44: Formation rules of arbitration agreements and ICSID arbitration rules", *Arbitration International* 36(1), 67–85 (2020),.

Muthucumaraswamy Sornarajah, "Power and justice in foreign investment arbitration", *Journal of International Arbitration* 14(3), 103–140 (1997).

Muthucumaraswamy Sornarajah, "The Retreat of Neo-Liberalism in Investment Treaty Arbitration", in Catherine A. Rogers, Roger P. Alford (eds.), *The Future of Investment Arbitration*, Oxford University Press, 2009, pp. 273–296.

Muthucumaraswamy Sornarajah, *The international law on foreign investment*, Cambridge University Press, 2021, pp. 291–339.

Nartnirun Junngam, "An MFN Clause and BIT Dispute Settlement: a Host State's Implied Consent to Arbitration by Reference", *UCLA Journal of International Law and Foreign Affairs* 15(2), 399–528 (2010).

Niccolò Ridi, "Approaches to External Precedent: The Invocation of International Jurisprudence in Investment Arbitration and WTO Dispute Settlement", in Szilárd Gáspár-Szilágyi, Daniel Behn, Malcolm Langford (eds.), *Adjudicating Trade and Investment Disputes: Convergence or Divergence?*, Cambridge University Press, 2020, pp. 121–148.

Niccolò Ridi, Thomas Schultz, *Empirically Mapping Investment Arbitration Scholarship: Networks, Authorities, and the Research Front*, Springer, 2021.

Nicolás M. Perrone, David Schneiderman, "International economic law's wreckage: depoliticization, inequality, precarity", in Emilios Christodoulidis, Ruth Dukes, Marco Goldoni (eds.), *Research Handbook on Critical Legal Theory*, Edward Elgar, 2019, pp. 446–472.

Nicolás M. Perrone, *Investment treaties and the legal Imagination: how foreign investors play by their own rules*, Oxford University Press, 2021.

Nicolle E. Kownacki, "Prospects for ICSID Arbitration in Post-Denunciation Countries: An Updated Approach", *UCLA Journal of International Law and Foreign Affairs* 15(2), 529–560 (2010).

Niki Nozari, *Applicable law in international arbitration: the experience of ICSID and Iran-United States Claims Tribunal*, Peter Lang, 2018.

Nitish Monebhurrun, Carolina Olarte-Bácares, Marco A. Velásquez-Ruiz, *International Investment Law and Arbitration from a Latin American Perspective*, Springer, 2024.

Noah Rubins, Bernhard Lauterburg, "Independence, Impartiality and Duty of Disclosure in Investment Arbitration", in Christina Knahr, Christian Koller, Walter Rechberger, August Reinisch (eds.), *Investment and Commercial Arbitration – Similarities and Divergences: Similarities and Divergences*, Eleven International Publishing, 2010, 153–180.

Okechukwu Emmanuel Wali, "A Contemporary Evaluation of Decisions and Approaches Shaping the Conceptualization of an 'ICSID Investment'", *Arbitration* 90(2), 224–257 (2024).

Oleksandra Vytiaganets, "Smoking Chills? Tobacco Regulatory Chill, Foreign Investment, and the NCD Crisis in the Post-Soviet Case: a Case Study from Ukraine", *The Journal of World Investment & Trade* 21(5), 753–780 (2020).

Omar E. García-Bolívar, "Comparing Arbitrator Standards of Conduct in International Commercial, Trade and Investment Disputes", *Dispute Resolution Journal* 60, 76–79 (2006).

Panagiotis Delimatsis, Georgios Dimitropoulos, Anastasios Gourgourinis (eds.), *State Capitalism and International Investment Law*, Hart, 2023.

Paolo Vargiu, "Beyond Hallmarks and Formal Requirements: a "Jurisprudence Constante" on the Notion of Investment in the ICSID Convention", *Journal of World Investment and Trade* 10(5), 753–768 (2009).

Paolo Vargiu, "Environmental Expropriation in International Investment Law", in Tullio Treves, Francesco Seatzu, Seline Trevisanut (eds.), *Foreign Investment, International Law and Common Concerns*, Routledge, 2014, pp. 213–238.

Paolo Vargiu, "*Langue* and *Parole* of Investment Law", *International Journal for the Semiotics of Law – Revue internationale de Sémiotique juridique* 36(1), 293–312 (2023).

Paolo Vargiu, "Stakeholders of Investment Arbitration: establishing a dialogue among arbitrators, states, investors, academics and other actors in international investment law", in Katia Fach Gómez (ed.), *Private Actors in International Investment Law*, Springer, 2021, pp. 5–25.

Paolo Vargiu, Francesco Seatzu, "Africanizing Bilateral Investment Treaties ('BITs'): Some Case Studies and Future Prospects of a Pro-Active African Approach to International Investment", *Connecticut Journal of International Law* 30(2), 143–168 (2015).

Paolo Vargiu, Francesco Seatzu, "Bilateralism, Multilateralism and the Quest for a Multilateral Investment Agreement for Sub-Saharan African Countries", *La Comunità Internazionale* 69(3), 315–340 (2014).

Paolo Vargiu, Francesco Seatzu, "Three Views of a Secret: Missed Opportunities in the ECHR's Recent Case-Law on International Commercial Arbitration", *The Italian Review of International and Comparative Law* 1(2), 1–21 (2022).

Pascale Accaoui Lorfing, Arnaud de Nanteuil, "Projet de code de conduite pour les arbitres dans les différends relatifs aux investissements internationaux – version deux", *Revue de droit des affaires internationals* 4, 581–585 (2021).

Patrick Dumberry, *A guide to general principles of law in international investment arbitration*, Oxford University Press, 2020.

Pedro Martinez-Fraga, Harout Jack Samra, "The Role of Precedent in Defining Res Judicata in Investor – State Arbitration", *Northwestern Journal of International Law & Business* 32(3), 419–450 (2012).

Peter D. Isakoff, "Defining the Scope of Indirect Expropriation for International Investments", *Global Business Law Review* 3(2), 189–210 (2013).

Peter L. Lindseth, "Theorizing Backlash: Supranational Governance and International Investment Law and Arbitration in Comparative Perspective", *Journal of World Investment & Trade* 21(1), 34–70 (2020).

Petra Butler, "Human Rights in International Commercial and Investment Arbitration", in Stefan Kröll, Andrea K. Bjorklund, Franco Ferrari, *Cambridge Compendium of International Commercial and Investment Arbitration*, Cambridge University Press, 2023, pp 139–185.

Phillip Landolt, "The Inconvenience of Principle: Separability and Kompetenz-Kompetenz", *Journal of International Arbitration* 30(5), 511–530 (2013).

Piero Bernardini, "Annulment of Awards", in Andrea Gattini, Attila Tanzi, and Filippo Fontanelli (eds.), *General Principles of Law and International Investment Arbitration*, Brill Nijhoff, 2018, pp. 168–188.

Pietro Ortolani, "Article 34: Application for Setting Aside as Exclusive Recourse against Arbitral Award", in Ilias Bantekas, Pietro Ortolani, Shahla Ali, Manuel A. Gomez, and Michael Polkinghorne, *UNCITRAL Model Law on International Commercial Arbitration: A Commentary*, Cambridge University Press, 2020, pp. 858–898.

Rafael Quintero Godinez, "A Case Note on the ICSID Tribunal's Decision in Hydro and Others v. Albania: Indirect Expropriation and Proportionality", *Journal of International Arbitration* 41(2), 225–250 (2024).

Rainer Hofmann, Stephan W. Schill, Christian J. Tams, *Preferential Trade and Investment Agreements – From Recalibration to Reintegration*, Nomos, 2013, p. 9.

Ramona Elisabeta Cîrlig, "The arbitral tribunal's authority to determine the applicable law in international commercial arbitration: patterns and trends", *Juridical Tribune* 9(1), 18–32 (2019).

Raphael Ren, The Dichotomy between Jurisdiction and Admissibility in International Arbitration, *International and Comparative Law Quarterly* 73(2), 417–446 (2024).

Relja Radović, *Beyond Consent: Revisiting Jurisdiction in Investment Treaty Arbitration*, Brill Nijhoff, 2021.

Richard C. Chen, "Precedent and dialogue in investment treaty arbitration", *Harvard International Law Journal* 60(1), 47–94 (2019).

Ridhi Kabra, "Has Abaclat v Argentina left the ICSID with a massive problem?", *Arbitration International* 31(3), 425–453 (2015).

Roland Kläger, *"Fair and equitable treatment" in International Investment Law*, Cambridge University Press, 2011.

Rowan Platt, "The appeal of appeal mechanisms in international arbitration: fairness over finality?", *Journal of International Arbitration* 30(5), 531–560 (2013).

Rumana Islam, *The Fair and Equitable Treatment (FET) standard in international investment arbitration: developing countries in context*, Springer, 2018.

Runar Hilleren Lie, "The Influence of Law Firms in Investment Arbitration", in Daniel Behn, Ole Kristian Fauchald, Malcolm Langford (eds.), *The Legitimacy of Investment Arbitration: Empirical Perspectives*, Cambridge University Press, 2022, pp. 100–132.

Santtu Turunen, "Arbitrators, Disclosure and Challenges: Are We Being Practical or Too Sensitive?", *Scandinavian Studies in Law* 63, 371–392 (2017).

Sarita Patil Woolhouse, "Transparency and Procedural Integrity of Arbitration – The Biwater Tribunal's Balancing Act", *Transnational Dispute Management* 5 (2006).

Sebastián López Escarcena, *Indirect expropriation in international law*, Edward Elgar, 2014.

Sergio M. Carbone, "Iura novit curia e arbitrato commerciale internazionale", *Rivista di Diritto Internazionale Privato e Processuale* 46(2), 353–366 (2010).

Sergio Puig, "Social capital in the arbitration market", *European Journal of International Law* 25(2), 387–424 (2014).

Sergio Puig, Anton Strezhnev, "Testing Cognitive Bias: Experimental Approaches and Investment Arbitration", in Daniel Behn, Ole Kristian Fauchald, Malcolm Langford (eds.), *The Legitimacy of Investment Arbitration: Empirical Perspectives*, Cambridge University Press, 2022, pp. 85–99.

Seung-Woon Lee, "Arbitrator's Evident Partiality: Current US Standards and Possible Solutions Based on Comparative Reviews", *Arbitration Law Review* 9(1), 159–176 (2017).

Sondra Faccio, "Investment Contracts and the Reform of Investment Arbitration: Towards Sustainability", *ICSID Review – Foreign Investment Law Journal* 38(3), 625–643 (2024).

Soterius Loizou, *Establishing the Content of the Applicable Law in International Arbitration*, Juris Publishing, 2019.

Stanimir A. Alexandrov, "Breach of Treaty Claims and Breach of Contract Claims: when can an International Tribunal exercise Jurisdiction?", in Katia Yannaca-Small (ed.), *Arbitration Under International Investment Agreements – A Guide to the Key Issues*, Oxford University Press, 2018, pp. 370–394.

Stanimir A. Alexandrov, "Breach of Treaty Claims and Breach of Contract Claims: is it still Unknown Territory?", in Katia Yannaca-Small (ed.), *Arbitration Under International Investment Agreements – A Guide to the Key Issues*, Oxford University Press, 2018, pp. 323–350.

Stavroula Angoura, *The Impartiality and Independence of Arbitrators in International Commercial Arbitration*, Nomos, 2022.

Stefan Kröll, Elian Keller, "The Competence-Competence Principle's Positive Effect", in Stefan Kröll, Andrea K. Bjorklund, Franco Ferrari, *Cambridge Compendium of International Commercial and Investment Arbitration*, Cambridge University Press, 2023, pp. 771–806.

Stefan Mandelbaum, "The Measure of Finality: A Dialectal Analysis of Legitimacy Concerns in International Investment Arbitration", *UCL Journal of Law and Jurisprudence* 9, 1–25 (2020).

Stefan Pislevik, "Precedent and development of law: Is it time for greater transparency in International Commercial Arbitration?", *Arbitration International* 34(2), 241–260 (2018).

Stephan W. Schill, "MFN Clauses as Bilateral Commitments to Multilateralism: a Reply to Simon Batifort and J. Benton Heath", American Journal of International Law 111(4), 914–935 (2017).

Stephan W. Schill, "Sources of international investment law: multilateralization, arbitral precedent, comparativism, soft law", in Jean d'Aspremont, Samantha Besson (eds.), *Oxford Handbook on the Sources of International Law*, Oxford University Press, 2018, pp. 1095–1115.

Stephan W. Schill, Geraldo Vidigal, "Designing investment dispute settlement à la carte: insights from comparative institutional design analysis", *The Law & Practice of International Courts and Tribunals* 18(3), 314–344 (2020).

Stephan W. Schill, *The Multilateralization of International Investment Law*, Cambridge University Press, 2009.

Stephen E. Blythe, "The Advantages of Investor-State Arbitration as a Dispute Resolution Mechanism in Bilateral Investment Treaties", *The International Lawyer* 47(2), 273–290 (2013).

Stephen J Toope, *Mixed International Arbitration: Studies in Arbitration between States and Private Persons*, Grotius, University of Cambridge, 1990.

Stephen M. Schwebel, "A BIT about ICSID", *ICSID Review – Foreign Investment Law Journal* 23(1), 1–9 (2008).

Steven R. Ratner, "International investment law through the lens of global justice", *Journal of International Economic Law* 20(4), 747–775 (2017).

Susan D. Franck, "Development and Outcomes of Investment Treaty Arbitration", *Harvard International Law Journal* 50(2), 435–490 (2009).

Susan D. Franck, "Rationalizing Costs in Investment Treaty Arbitration", *Washington University Law Review* 88(4), 769–852 (2011).

Susan D. Franck, "The role of international arbitrators", *ILSA Journal of International & Comparative Law* 12(2), 499–522 (2006).

Susan D. Franck, Anne van Aaken, James Freda, Chris Guthrie, Jeffrey J. Rachlinski, "Inside the Arbitrator's Mind", *Emory Law Journal* 66(5), 1115–1174 (2017).

Susan D. Franck, James Freda, Kellen Lavin, Tobias Kellen, Anne van Aaken, "The Diversity Challenge: Exploring the Invisible College of International Arbitration", *Columbia Journal of Transnational Law* 53(3), 429–506 (2015).

Tania Voon, Andrew D. Mitchell, "Denunciation, termination and survival: the interplay of treaty law and international investment law", *ICSID Review – Foreign Investment Law Journal* 31(2), 413–433 (2016).

Tanjina Sharmin, Emmanuel Laryea, "Application of MFN to investment dispute settlement: rule of law issues", *Journal of International Trade Law and Policy* 20(1), 21–41 (2021).

Tarald Laudal Berge, Axel Berger, "Do Investor-State Dispute Settlement Cases Influence Domestic Environmental Regulation? The Role of Respondent State Bureaucratic Capacity", *Journal of International Dispute Settlement* 12(1), 1–41 (2021).

Thomas D. Grant, F. Scott Kieff, "Appointing Arbitrators: Tenure, Public Confidence, and a Middle Road for ISDS Reform", *Michigan Journal of International Law* 43(1), 171–239 (2022).

Thomas Schultz, "Against consistency in investment arbitration", in Zachary Douglas, Joost Pauwelyn, and Jorge E. Vinuales (eds.), *The Foundations of International Investment Law – Bringing Theory into Practice*, Oxford University Press, 2014, pp. 297–316.

Thomas Schultz, Cedric Dupont, "Investment arbitration: Promoting the rule of law or over-empowering investors?:A quantitative empirical study", *European Journal of International Law* 25(4), 1147–1168 (2014).

Thomas Schultz, Niccolò Ridi, "Arbitration literature", in Thomas Schultz, Federico Ortino (eds.), *Oxford Handbook of International Arbitration*, Oxford University Press, 2020, pp. 1–32.

Thomas W. Walsh, "Substantive Review of ICSID Awards: Is the Desire for Accuracy Sufficient to Compromise Finality?", *Berkeley Journal of International Law* 24(2), 444–462 (2006).

Tim A. Hagemann, "The North-South Divide of Regulatory Chill: A Comparative Analysis of the Impact of Investor-State Dispute Settlement on Policy Makers in Developed and Developing Countries", *New York International Law Review* 35(1), 27–48 (2022).

Timothy Foden, Odysseas G. Repousis, "Giving away home field advantage: the misguided attack on confidentiality in international commercial arbitration", *Arbitration International* 35(4), 401–418 (2019).

Tony Cole (ed.), *The Roles of Psychology in International Arbitration*, Wolters Kluwer, 2017.

Velimir Živković, *Fair and equitable treatment and the rule of law*, Edward Elgar, 2023.

Vera Korzum, "Enforcing soft law in international investment arbitration", *Vanderbilt Journal of Transnational Law* 56(1), 1–65 (2023).

Vitalius Tumonis, "Judicial Creativity and Constraint of Legal Rules: Dueling Cannons of International Law", *University of Miami International & Comparative Law Review* 20(1), 93–133 (2012).

Walter Mattli, "Private justice in a global economy: from litigation to arbitration", *International Organization* 55(4), 919–947 (2001).

Wei Shen, "Is This a Great Leap Forward? A Comparative Review of the Investor-State Arbitration Clause in the ASEAN-China Investment Treaty: From BIT Jurisprudential and Practical Perspectives", *Journal of International Arbitration* 7(4), 379–419 (2010).

Wei Sun, "A New Test Toward Consistency in International Investment Arbitration", *ICSID Review – Foreign Investment Law Journal* 39(1), 121–138 (2024)

William A. Schabas, Shannonbrooke Murphy (eds.), *Research Handbook on International Courts and Tribunals*, Edward Elgar, 2017.

William Knull, Noah Robins, "Betting the Farm on International Arbitration: Is It Time to Offer an Appeal Option?" *The American Review of International Arbitration* 11, 531–577 (2000).

William W. Park, "The Arbitrability Dicta in *First Options v. Kaplan*: What Sort of Kompetenz-Kompetenz Has Crossed the Atlantic?", *Arbitration International* 12(2), 137–160 (1996).

William W. Park, Jan Paulsson, "The Binding Force of International Arbitral Awards", *Virginia Journal of International Law* 23(2), 253–286 (1983).

Wim Naudé, "Entrepreneurship, developing countries, and development economics: new approaches and insights, *Small Business Economics* 34, 1–12 (2010).

Wolfgang Alschner, "Ensuring Correctness or Promoting Consistency? Tracking Policy Priorities in Investment Arbitration through Large-Scale Citation Analysis", *Ottawa Faculty of Law Working Paper 2019-42* (2019).

Wolfgang Alschner, *Investment Arbitration and State-Driven Reform: New Treaties, Old Outcomes*, Oxford University Press, 2022.

Yas Banifatemi, Emmanuel Gaillard, "The Long March towards a Jurisprudence Constante on the Notion of Investment, Salini v. Morocco, ICSID Case No ARB/00/4," in Meg Kinnear, Geraldine R. Fischer, Jara Minguez Almeida, Luisa Fernanda Torres, Mairée Uran Bidegain (eds.), *Building International Investment Law – The First 50 Years of ICSID*, Wolters Kluwer, 2014, pp. 97–125.

Yuval Shany, "Contract Claims vs. Treaty Claims: Mapping Conflicts between ICSID Decisions on Multisourced Investment Claims", *American Journal of International Law* 99(4), 835–851 (2005).

Zachary Douglas, "Can a doctrine of precedent be justified in investment treaty arbitration?", *ICSID Review – Foreign Investment Law Journal* 25(1), 104–110 (2010).

Zachary Douglas, "The MFN Clause in Investment Arbitration: Treaty Interpretation Off the Rails", *Journal of International Dispute Settlement* 2(1), 97–113 (2011).

Zuzana Jahodníková, Ludovít Mičinský, "Crossing the Rubicon – on the Correlation of the Principle of Transparency and Confidentiality of Arbitral Proceedings within the Area of International Investment Arbitration: Does Investment Arbitration have the Credentials to trump the Principle of Confidentiality in Arbitration?", *Czech Yearbook of Public & Private International Law* 3, 239–261 (2012).

INDEX